eBay Income Advanced:

How to Take Your eBay Business to the Next Level — For PowerSellers and Beyond

By John N. Peragine, Jr.

eBay Income Advanced: How to Take Your eBay Business to the Next Level — For PowerSellers and Beyond

1405 SW 6th Avenue • Ocala, Florida 34471 • Phone 800-814-1132 • Fax 352-622-1875
Web site: www.atlantic-pub.com • E-mail: sales@atlantic-pub.com
SAN Number: 268-1250

ISBN-13: 978-1-60138-123-1 ISBN-10: 1-60138-123-9

Library of Congress Cataloging-in-Publication Data

Peragine, John N., 1970-
EBay income advanced : how to take your eBay business to the next level--for powersellers and beyond / by John N. Peragine, Jr.
p. cm.
Includes bibliographical references and index.
ISBN-13: 978-1-60138-123-1 (alk. paper)
ISBN-10: 1-60138-123-9 (alk. paper)
1. eBay (Firm) 2. Internet auctions. 3. Electronic commerce. I. Title.
HF5478.P468 2009
658.8'7--dc22
2009012602

Printed in the United States

PROJECT MANAGER: Melissa Peterson • mpeterson@atlantic-pub.com
COVER DESIGN: Meg Buchner • megadesn@mchsi.com
INTERIOR DESIGN: Holly Marie Gibbs • hgibbs@atlantic-pub.com

We recently lost our beloved pet "Bear," who was not only our best and dearest friend but also the "Vice President of Sunshine" here at Atlantic Publishing. He did not receive a salary but worked tirelessly 24 hours a day to please his parents. Bear was a rescue dog that turned around and showered myself, my wife Sherri, his grandparents Jean, Bob and Nancy and every person and animal he met (maybe not rabbits) with friendship and love. He made a lot of people smile every day.

We wanted you to know that a portion of the profits of this book will be donated to The Humane Society of the United States. ***–Douglas & Sherri Brown***

The human-animal bond is as old as human history. We cherish our animal companions for their unconditional affection and acceptance. We feel a thrill when we glimpse wild creatures in their natural habitat or in our own backyard.

Unfortunately, the human-animal bond has at times been weakened. Humans have exploited some animal species to the point of extinction.

The Humane Society of the United States makes a difference in the lives of animals here at home and worldwide. The HSUS is dedicated to creating a world where our relationship with animals is guided by compassion. We seek a truly humane society in which animals are respected for their intrinsic value, and where the human-animal bond is strong.

Want to help animals? We have plenty of suggestions. Adopt a pet from a local shelter, join The Humane Society and be a part of our work to help companion animals and wildlife. You will be funding our educational, legislative, investigative and outreach projects in the U.S. and across the globe.

Or perhaps you'd like to make a memorial donation in honor of a pet, friend or relative? You can through our Kindred Spirits program. And if you'd like to contribute in a more structured way, our Planned Giving Office has suggestions about estate planning, annuities, and even gifts of stock that avoid capital gains taxes.

Maybe you have land that you would like to preserve as a lasting habitat for wildlife. Our Wildlife Land Trust can help you. Perhaps the land you want to share is a backyard—that's enough. Our Urban Wildlife Sanctuary Program will show you how to create a habitat for your wild neighbors.

So you see, it's easy to help animals. And The HSUS is here to help.

THE HUMANE SOCIETY OF THE UNITED STATES.

2100 L Street NW • Washington, DC 20037 • 202-452-1100 • www.hsus.org

DEDICATION

I dedicate this book to my loving wife, two beautiful daughters, Teeny and Izze. This book is part of my legacy to them.

Table of Contents

Open Doors by Raising Your "Status" Quo 159

Streamlining Your Finances 167

Going Beyond eBay 183

Advertise, Advertise, Advertise 195

Finding the Best Products for the Cheapest Prices 227

Work Smarter, Not Harder 253

Developing and Using a Business Plan 261

FOREWORD

Congratulations on your decision to start an eBay business! Starting your business can be one of the most stressful and exciting experiences of your life. Leaving the security of a paying job and jumping into the world of entrepreneurship can cause any normal person to miss a few nights sleep. Your friends and family may be helping the insomnia by telling you that you are crazy to take such risks in today's economy.

You may have started out on eBay by selling a few things that were collecting dust around the house and after a few sales you have realized the potential and are ready to harness it. Many of us enjoy the thrill of reading those "you've got cash" e-mails as we drink our morning coffee. There isn't anything more exciting than knowing you made money while you slept! Really, the grass is pretty green in these early days of Internet commerce. Each year, as the small mom and pop stores disappear from Main Street, new ones are popping up in the new virtual 'Mall of America' called eBay.

Some eBay sellers have grown and experienced the freedom of being their own boss, others have failed miserably and are going back to the nine to five routine disillusioned and broke. The failure rate for retailers is high, even with the enhanced opportunity for small business owners on eBay.

That's because selling on eBay seems to be such a revolutionary way to conduct business that many people forget the basics. A start-up must have a business and marketing plan, enough capital to buy opening inventory, business licenses, and considerations about how and where you to conduct your business. You must have a road map for your business clearly thought out long before you take open the virtual doors. If you do not you are very likely to fail within your first few months.

I am not telling you these things to scare you back into that cubical-walled world – I am writing about them to congratulate you for choosing eBay Income Advanced to help you get started. Author John Peragine walks you through the necessary steps to starting a business. He includes chapters on:

- How and what to write in a business plan
- How to calculate your selling margins
- How to figure out if your business is sound and making a profit
- When, where and how to deal with your stock
- Shipping tips and techniques
- The automation tools necessary to running a day-to-day eBay business
- How to list an item for sale on eBay
- How to find inventory – to keep your shelves stocked
- Sage advice on drop-shipping and other 'too good to be true' offers
- Information about being a trading assistant
- Much more on the routine of running an eBay PowerSelling business

eBay Income Advanced is a primer on how to take your eBay business to the next level and ramp it up to PowerSeller status – step-by-step. By reading this book, you are taking the first steps toward creating a lasting business on eBay. Remembering the fundamentals of business, you will know when to take the necessary steps towards growth and when to avoid unnecessary risks.

The greatest asset of eBay is its enormous size. That size is also its biggest drawback for the individual seller. How do you attract new business when you are a needle in a haystack? Every successful business owner knows how important it is to bring in new customers and keep the ones you have sold to coming back for more. John Peragine explains the basics of marketing to your customers.

I suggest you to keep this book near your computer as you continue to explore and grow your business. It is my hope that you are successful beyond your wildest dreams. I know this is a guidebook designed to show you how to build your enterprise and reach your goals. Once you have the nuts and bolts mastered, I encourage you to continue to grow your business. Continue reading every business book you can get your hands on; study eBay marketing, budgets, and even the legal guides. If you continue to study and learn, I know you will master the art of making money on eBay.

Cindy Shebley
eBay Certified Business Consultant
Author of *The eBay Marketing Bible*
www.clovercity.com

Cindy Shebley is an eBay Certified Business Consultant, Education Specialist and author who teaches throughout the Northwest. Shebley's eBay career started in the late 90s as a way to liquidate inventory from her "bricks and mortar" store. Today, Shebley is an eBay PowerSeller who sells photography, video equipment, and supplies for eBay sellers.

As an eBay Certified Business Consultant, Shebley helps clients grow their businesses and teaches them the marketing techniques needed to stay competitive in today's marketplace. Shebley is the author of several books on eBay, including Easy Auction Photography, How To Squidoo, and Five

Steps To Success: Growing your Online Business and Increasing Your Profits.

Shebley hosts Add Video to Your eBay Listings a DVD course produced by Ghost Leg Media.

Currently, Shebley is writing a marketing guide for eBay sellers called The eBay Marketing Bible, which will be released early in 2009. More information about her can be found at www.clovercity.com.

INTRODUCTION

Thousands of people go to eBay every day trying to find that special something, that magical "it" that is going to make everything better. More people have begun to value Internet commerce over traditional "go to the store and buy it" shopping.

It is easy to see why. The advantages of eBay over traditional forms of commerce are obvious. No lines, no screaming children, and no driving from store to store to make sure you are getting the lowest price possible. In short, shopping online provides the most stress-free, rewarding shopping experience possible, and as more of the world is becoming computer savvy, the online marketplace is expanding at light speed.

All you need to do to buy something online is to go to eBay or do an online search for whatever it is that you are looking for, and you will get many pages of search results. Most of the results for items through search engines such as Google will still result in links to **eBay.com**. Actually, eBay has become such a trusted brand that many people skip the search engines altogether and log on directly to **eBay.com**.

Tips from the Experts

I hate to be flip, but the bottom line is that it is strictly the dollar amount sold. What sets a regular seller apart from a great Power-Seller is customer service.

— Charlene Anderson

On eBay's search engine, you can sort your search by quality (new or used) and price. You have the option of selecting whom you want to buy from and how fast do you want the item (shipping options), and presto, you are done. What would have taken hours of shopping around has just taken you about two minutes.

Many have been able to cash in on this opportunity and hundreds have been able to quit their day jobs by devoting themselves to eBay full-time. This transition does not just happen by itself, so before you quit your day job, read this book.

Creating a successful eBay business and becoming a PowerSeller takes plenty of time and energy. It takes knowledge, skill, know-how, expert advice, and considerable research. If you are already a business-savvy person, and you treat your eBay venture like the business opportunity it is, then chances are, you will do extremely well.

Thomas Edison, the famed inventor of the light bulb, once said, "Genius is 1 percent inspiration, and 99 percent perspiration." Edison worked tirelessly trying to produce a light bulb — something that he believed was theoretically possible, though it had not yet been done. Through sheer force of will and an iron determination, he refused to quit after failing countless times. He persevered all because of that tiny bit of inspiration; that little bit of insight that told him that his dreams might just be possible.

Tips from the Experts

A PowerSeller has to give customer service to keep at that level. In my case, to keep my PowerSeller level requires a lot of sales because I deal in small-dollar media items. I am not like some who can keep PowerSeller status by selling one or two high-dollar items. My average item sells for $5to $10, so I need to sell 150 items a month to compete at the lowest level of PowerSeller.

— Jim Stewart

To be successful as an eBay PowerSeller takes plenty of hard work and a tiny bit of inspiration that will tell you that your dreams, too, are possible. That inspiration, even if it is small when compared to the amount of work you will do, is vital, and without it, there is no drive to keep going when times get tough. This book can inspire you for years to come.

My advice is to read this book straight through. Then, keep it by your computer and use it as a reference book, turning to the relevant material as needed. Knowledge is useless if it is not applied. This is not the type of book that should be left on a shelf.

This book is my gift to you after spending thousands of hours talking to eBay experts who are successful every day doing what many people only dream of doing — making a fortune through their own personal eBay success story. The next success story could be yours.

This book is for those who have already gotten the basics of eBay business under their belts. This book is a complete volume that helps transform the beginner into a PowerSeller. You will find that becoming a PowerSeller is not as hard as staying a PowerSeller. The advice given here will give you that edge and staying power.

Thomas Edison's story has become almost a modern-day fable, teaching timeless lessons on the value of perseverance and not giving up, giving inspiration for countless other dreamers like him. He once remarked, after finally succeeding and being catapulted to international fame, "I have not failed. I've just found 10,000 ways that won't work." But some of his critics and colleagues argued that it did not have to be as hard on Edison as it was.

A contemporary of Edison, Nicola Tesla, once noted about his fellow friend and scientist:

"If Edison had a needle to find in a haystack, he would proceed at once with the diligence of the bee to examine straw after straw until he found the object of his search... I was a sorry witness of such doings, knowing that a little theory and calculation would have saved him 90 percent of his labor."

Tesla is regarded by many as the greatest electrical engineer of his time, and his theories helped usher in what came to be called the Second Industrial Revolution. He regarded Edison as a success story, but argued that success might have come much easier to him if he had listened to people who could have taught him that little bit of theory and calculation that he lacked.

Tesla argued that what Edison could have learned from others would have saved him years of aggravation and needless suffering. Being successful on eBay is essentially the same. You try by yourself to figure out all the things you are going to have to do to be successful with your online store. You can have sleepless nights, failures, and upsets before finally getting some amount of success for all your trials and labors. Or you can learn from those who have made all the mistakes before and learned how to be successful. They are living testimonies to the power of following your dreams. They are doing what thousands only dream of doing, every day of their lives.

This book is an invaluable tool that will save you time, money, and resources; it is the "little bit of theory and calculation" that will save you precious time and labor. Learn from it. Even if you have already managed to succeed in the eBay arena, you can use this book to become even more successful. Or even better, to learn some tricks of the trade to make your business run smoother and easier, freeing up time that you could be devoting to other things.

Use the knowledge within these pages to drive yourself to PowerSeller status and beyond. Some of the information can be found on **eBay.com**, but I have attempted to give you as much of the relevant information as possible in this book. Sometimes it can be difficult to surf through help pages to find the answers to your questions. Since some of the material can change quickly, I also provide you the Web page to go to find the most current updates.

CHAPTER 1

What PowerSelling Means

Tips from the Experts

Convincing the big wholesalers I was a serious business, even though I didn't have a brick-and-mortar store, was my biggest difficulty. Once I broke through and convinced them I had a serious business, things fell into place. I have found that I can source from any supplier in my field. It took the two "big guys" in the business to say "yes" to me to open all the doors. So don't give up on that first "no." If I had, I wouldn't have my business. I found a way that was a win/win for both of us. Find a way to work with the wholesaler so it works for both of you.

— Charlene Anderson

Tips from the Experts

The pursuit of maximum profit, fewest hours spent working, and happy customers. I'm always looking to improve on those three factors.

— Jim Cockrum

Tips from the Experts

Any seller can do the volume necessary to achieve PowerSeller status. The trick is keeping it. You must run your business with professionalism and treat your customers with respect.

— Tom Orr

Becoming a PowerSeller is not as hard as you may think. If you sell on eBay on a regular basis, you can attain the status of a PowerSeller. The staff at eBay does a good job of monitoring accounts and reviewing them to see if they are eligible for PowerSeller performance on a monthly basis. The gross sales are assessed on a monthly basis. Once the eligibility threshold is met, an eBay seller will receive an e-mail indicated that they have reached PowerSeller status.

PowerSelling Tip

If you are concerned about getting your notification of PowerSeller status, you can go to the opt-in setting on your "My eBay" page. This will allow you to receive notifications about being a PowerSeller by any means you wish, such as e-mail, snail mail, or telephone.

There are several rules to becoming a PowerSeller, and they are as follows:

- You have to have been an active seller on eBay for at least 90 days.
- You must have sold on average a minimum of two items on eBay per month for the past three consecutive months. You must also maintain a minimum of four average monthly listings for the past three months. In addition to the monthly requirement, you must have also sold and average of two items per month for the past twelve months.

- You need to have, at minimum, an overall feedback rating of 100.
- Your feedback ratings must have an average of 98 or above.
- Your Detailed Seller Rating (DSR) must have stayed at 4.5 or above for the past 12 months in all 4 classification ratings.
- Your eBay Seller's account must be current, which means that you must pay your bill to eBay on time.
- You must be in compliance with eBay's listing policies on their site.
- Your eBay business must be in sync with eBay's community values.
- You must have sold an average of $1,000 in gross merchandise sales or at least 100 items a month for the prior three months through eBay or its affiliates: **half.com**, eBay express, or eBay motors. In addition, there is an annual requirement of a minimum of $12,000 or 1,200 items for the prior twelve months.

PowerSelling Tip

eBay uses total feedback when looking at PowerSeller Feedback and DSRs. PowerSeller Feedback uses this formula:

$$\frac{\textit{Total Number of positive feedback}}{\textit{Total Number of possible feedback (Positive and Negative)}}$$

Some of the requirements seem obvious, while others may need a further explanation and more in-depth work. Being an active seller for 90 days means having an active, paid-up account for three months. There is not much you can do to improve that area; you just have to wait.

You have to make sure that you have sold a minimum of two items per month for the prior three months and for the past twelve months. This may seem like it is the same requirement, but it is not. It is much harder to average two items per month for three months than to average two items per month for twelve months. You can have a bad month during a year and make it up over the next few months. If you have a bad month during a three-month period, it is hard to make it up. The key is the three consecutive months. This can occur at anytime, but must fall during a year when your sales are pretty even. Keep an eye on how many listings you are posting because it is just as important as sales for PowerSeller eligibility.

The truth is that you need to be selling much more than the aforementioned minimum, unless you are selling high-priced items, like cars or homes. If you are not meeting this minimum amount, you might want to look at what it is you are selling and decide whether it is a truly viable product.

You have to have a 100 feedback rating and an average rating of 98 percent. You will learn throughout this book that customer service is the key to becoming a PowerSeller and maintaining that status. Do not allow a bad feedback to go by without trying to resolve the issues to the best of your ability.

Detailed Seller Rating

A DSR is an indicator of customer satisfaction. A recent addition to eBay is the ability for buyers to leave an anonymous rating of your businesses performance in four different areas: items as described, communication, shipping time, and shipping charges. A buyer can leave these ratings without you knowing who left it. The ratings use stars 1-5. DSR will not affect your ratings, but it can affect your eBay reputation and is essential in your quest to become a PowerSeller. A rating is an overall feeling your customer has about their experience with you. DSR includes more specific areas that can give you an idea of where you need improvement.

You will learn how to boost each of these areas. You need to look at them from time to time and look for any trends. You want the average in each area to be at least 4.5 stars in order to meet the eligibility requirements to become a PowerSeller.

Here are some tips to help you keep your DSR scores where they need to be:

- **Item Description:** In this area, you need to be careful how you are describing your items. You must be totally honest and describe your items as accurately as possible. You may think that by adding information or not being totally honest, will win you a sale. While in the short-term, someone may buy the item, this practice can completely undermine your reputation as a seller. A particular word to be careful about is "new." "New" should never be used to describe almost new, refurbished, or used items. New items have never been used before and are in their original package.

- **Communication:** If you are like many sellers, you might not check your e-mail on the weekends. This is perfectly acceptable, as working all the time can lead to burn out. If this is the case, be sure to let your buyers know your business hours. You should also encourage your buyers to only evaluate your communication skills based upon your response time on weekdays, as this is a more accurate evaluation.

- **Shipping Time:** Remind your buyers that shipping time is not the same as transit time. In order for them to accurately give you a score, they should look at the post mark on your package rather than when it arrived. It is important to let your buyers know when you ship; drop them a line when you have actually sent their package, and be diligent about sending packages quickly. Remind the buyers that you are not responsible for delays in transit or the time it takes for their payment to clear, as the latter will affect when you will ship a package. Maintaining open, frequent communication about shipping will often increase your average score in this area.

- **Shipping Charges:** In a later chapter, you will learn more in-depth ways to control your shipping charges. It is the handling charges that buyers sometimes miss. It is normal to charge a fee for packing supplies and boxes, and this is over and above the cost of shipping. You should have your handling charges and policies written clearly where your buyers can see them. This can help you avoid any problems and can increase your average score in this area.

eBay Bill

You must pay attention to when eBay sends you a bill for the fees you have accrued. You have a few options for payment. You can either pay your fees by making a separate payment every month, or you can set up an automatic draft from a credit card, checking account, or eBay. If you are sure your funds will be available, you should choose the automatic debit because you will always be on time that way. If you do not pay your fees, your account can be suspended, which can cost you money and set you back in your pursuit of a PowerSeller status.

eBay sends you an invoice for what you owe monthly, and you can view this under My eBay under the account tab. Keep an eye on this, as your fees can add up quickly.

eBay Listing Policies

It is crucial that you follow the eBay listing policies. If you violate this rule, the following can happen:

- Your listing can be cancelled
- eBay can place limits on your account privileges
- Your seller account can be suspended
- You could be asked to pay eBay fees on cancelled listings

- You can lose your PowerSeller status

You can find a list of eBay Policies at **http://pages.eBay.com/help/policies/listing-ov.html**. Look at these from time to time, as the policies can change. In addition, you should also look at the restricted items list at **http://pages.eBay.com/help/policies/items-ov.html**. Before you ever decide to list a new item in your store or on eBay, you should make sure that it is not on the restricted items list. The other page you should review and know is the intellectual properties page, **http://pages.eBay.com/help/tp/programs-vero-ov.html**. You need to make sure that selling your items does not violate any of these policies.

Community Values

eBay has become so large and so much a part of people's lives that an "eBay Community" has formed. It is a mini society and, therefore, must have rules. These rules are simple and relatively easy to follow. They are logical and follow good business practices. Violating these values will prevent you from attaining the PowerSeller status, and, in some circumstances, it can lead to the suspension of your account. There are only five fundamental values listed on the site, and they are as follows:

1. We believe people are basically good

2. We believe everyone has something to contribute

3. We believe that an honest, open environment can bring out the best in people

4. We recognize and respect everyone as a unique individual

5. We encourage you to treat others the way you want to be treated

Gross Sales

Being a PowerSeller is a privilege that is given to the small percentage of sellers on eBay that strive to sell a higher number of products and are grossing more money than many of their competitors. If they gave this status to everyone, it would not mean much to buyers when they see that logo on a listing or store site.

Selling $1,000 a month and an average of $12,000 a year is the minimum amount required to become a PowerSeller. As far as a full-time business goes, this is not much. At this rate, your business may not exist long because you will not be making enough money to live on. Once you read this book and start using the tips and techniques suggested, you will find your business tripling and quadrupling in sales.

Congratulations, You Made It

If you ever played king of the mountain as a kid, you might remember that making it to the top is not half as hard as staying at the top. Becoming a PowerSeller is just your first step toward becoming a thriving, money-making entity on eBay. You must continue to work hard and set your goals even higher.

eBay reviews PowerSeller eligibility every month once you become a PowerSeller. Here are their requirements for keeping your PowerSeller status.

- You must continue to uphold the eBay's community values
- You must continue to be in good financial standing with eBay
- You must continue to sell, on average, a minimum of two items on eBay per month
- Your feedback ratings must continue to have a monthly average of 98 percent or above

- Your DSR must stay at 4.5, or above average, every month in all four classification areas
- You must continue to be in compliance with eBay's listing policies on their site
- Your eBay business must continue to be in sync with eBay's community values
- You must continue to sell an average of $1,000 in gross merchandise sales or an average of 100 items a month.

If you fall below the level of eligibility, you will receive an alert communication. You will then have 30 days to improve the areas that are lacking in order to continue your PowerSeller status.

Membership has Benefits

You have finally made it and have been granted PowerSeller status. Following are the benefits that come with making it to the top.

- You will receive priority customer service, whether it is by e-mail or phone. At certain PowerSeller tiers, you will be assigned an account manager.
- You will receive discounts on Final Value Fees based on your DSRs.
- You will receive the benefit of unpaid item protection for Feature Fees.
- If you use PayPal, you will receive expanded seller protection on items paid through them.
- Based upon DSRs, you will have increased visibility in Best Match searches.

- You can nominate your favorite charities to receive donations through the Powerful Giving program.

- You will receive exclusive offers from third parties.

- You will receive access to PowerSeller-only networking boards.

- You can receive up to a 23 percent discount on UPS Ground Daily Rates.

Beyond the benefits that eBay gives you, the PowerSeller icon is like a money magnet. Buyers know that you are not just selling junk out of a garage. They know that you have sold many items and that your customer satisfaction rating is high. There may be many other sellers that are selling similar products to yours, but being a PowerSeller gives you a distinct advantage.

When a buyer goes online, they want three things:

1. The lowest price

2. The best-quality product

3. Exceptional customer service

Having that PowerSeller icon displayed assures them that they will receive all three.

Levels within PowerSelling

There are five tiers that a PowerSeller can achieve. In order to move up to the next tier, a PowerSeller must continue to achieve the monthly criteria and reach the next tier's minimum average monthly sales or items sold. Here is a breakdown of each tier and its sales requirement. These requirements can be met on **eBay.com**, **Half.com**, and eBay Motors.

- Bronze $1,000 or 100 items sold
- Silver $3,000 or 300 items sold
- Gold $10,000 or 1,000 items sold
- Platinum $25,000 or 2,500 items sold
- Titanium $150,000 or 15,000 items sold

As with the other requirements of remaining a PowerSeller, if the average number falls, then the PowerSeller will descend back down the tiers.

You should now have a good grasp on what the eligibility requirements are to be a PowerSeller and what is expected of you once you reach that level. The next chapter will discuss common pitfalls, and ways to avoid them, on eBay.

CHAPTER 2

Pitfalls to Avoid

There are a number of pitfalls you should avoid in order to keep your PowerSeller status. There are certain policies within eBay that you will learn about in this chapter. I have not listed all the policies on eBay, just the ones that a seller may unwittingly violate in their pursuit of money and more buyers. Violating these policies is never worth the risk of losing your PowerSeller status or your ability to do business on eBay. The policies protect you and your buyers. Having an honest business will win you more buyers than trying to cheat the system will.

Keyword Spamming

In a later chapter, you will learn about different marketing techniques. I have included keyword spamming here because it is a serious violation of eBay policies and must be avoided. Let's say you want to promote your store in every one of your auction listings. That is a good thing to do, but you have to be sure you do not engage in what is known as "keyword spamming." In short, your invitation to view your store cannot refer to your store items by their brand names, or even their keywords. Your invitation must be generic in nature. You cannot say "Be sure to view my store for more great items, including purses by Louis Vuitton, Manolo Blahnik, Gucci, and more!" Even if that particular auction is for one of those designer purses, you cannot list other brand names in your auction text, not even in an invitation to view your store or other auctions.

Let's say your auction is for a Gucci purse; the invitation to your store can say, "Be sure to visit my store for more great designer items," as this does not mention purses or any particular designer or brand name.

This is a big issue on eBay because an unscrupulous seller will insert popular keywords in his auction text so that when a looker searches "Manolo Blahnik," the seller's auction will show up in the search results, even though their auction has nothing to do with that keyword. They do this in an attempt to gain more exposure for their items.

This practice is unfair to the searcher who is not interested in the item being misrepresented, and it seriously affects the integrity of eBay's database and search results. Although eBay is constantly on the lookout for violations of this policy, it cannot be all places at all times. It is up to all sellers to be aware of this underhanded method of promoting listings and make a commitment never to engage in it. Promote your store in a way that showcases your integrity as a seller. Buyers look for and appreciate honest, trustworthy sellers.

When you use appropriate cross-promotions to attract buyers to your store, they merely have to glance at the left-hand side of the screen to see the neatly categorized list of all your items. Perhaps they are not interested in spare bike parts, but you have also picked up a nice wholesale lot of porcelain dolls. If they see a category for porcelain dolls, they can avoid paging through all your items and go straight to what they are interested in.

Shill Bidding

Suppose you found a hideous porcelain bowl in your attic. You do your research and find that it is only worth about $400. You have seen other bowls selling for even more on eBay. As the bidding proceeds, it does not seem like anyone is seeing the bowl for what it is worth, so you ask your brother to start bidding to make the price higher. You are hoping that if other bidders are seeing the bid go higher, they will see that the item is worth more.

The problem with this scenario is that this practice is called "shill bidding" and it violates the policies of eBay. It is an unfair practice of price inflation. eBay feels that relatives, friends, and employees have an unfair access to the item and therefore cannot bid. Even if their intent is to buy the item for their own use, it is still prohibited and could cost you your PowerSeller status. The only way they can buy your items is to use the Buy It Now option. It may also be tempting to use shilling practices to make your sales look higher than they are by having someone you know buy items that they never get or pay for.

The solution to your problem is better marketing and better descriptions of your products. If you have good customer ratings, products, and service, people will buy your goods at a fair price. If you find that you are tempted to use shill bidding practices, you need to rethink your strategic plan. Use the tips found in this book to improve your listings. If you find that something is not selling, let it go and move on to products that will sell. Use poorly performing items as a guide to determine your selling practices.

eBay is rather generous in its forgiveness of policy violations before they take away your PowerSeller status. The higher the tier you are in, the more forgiving they are.

Bronze	4 violations in a 60-day period
Silver/Gold	5 violations in a 60-day period
Platinum	6 violations in a 60-day period
Titanium	7 violations in a 60-day period

Excessive Shipping and Handling

In the first chapter, you learned that shipping and handling charges are part of the DSR evaluation. Beyond that, eBay has a policy against excessive shipping and handling charges. I have dedicated a whole chapter to shipping and ways to make your shipping and handling charges more efficient, but here, I have listed areas that could cause you to violate eBay policies.

eBay relies on customer reports and their own observations about whether a seller is charging unreasonable shipping and handling charges.

- You cannot list shipping and handling fees as a percentage of the final price.

- The only things that your charges may include are the actual shipping cost and a reasonable handling fee. A seller can offer extra services and insurance for a separate fee but cannot include them in the normal shipping and handling fees.

- The following charges are not allowed in your shipping and handling fees: tax (except applicable fees such as Federal State, local, and VAT tax); additional insurance; tariffs and duties (buyer may be responsible for paying fees, but the seller does not collect them); extra fees, such as gasoline, mileage, or time spent packing; PayPal fees; or eBay fees.

- If you list free shipping to anywhere or to particular destinations as part of your listing, you cannot charge any shipping or handling fees for those destinations.

Accepted Payment Methods

In October of 2008, eBay enacted new rules about the accepted payment options that can be offered. Sellers must now offer at least one of the following payment methods:

- PayPal

- Credit or debit card processed through an Internet merchant account

- ProPay

Sellers can also offer, but are not required to offer, the following payment options. These are only allowed in specific categories listed on the eBay site. If they are not in the approved categories, then the seller cannot use these types of payments:

- Bank-to-bank transfers
- Checks
- Money orders
- Any of the following online payment services: Allpay.net, cash2india, CertaPay, Checkfree.com, hyperwallet.com, Moneybookers.com, Nochex.com, Ozpay.biz, Paymate.com.au, and XOOM

It is important to make sure that you post the appropriate payment methods on your site and your auctions. Here is a list of payment methods a seller cannot request:

- Cash through the mail
- Cash or money orders through instant cash transfer services, such as Western Union or MoneyGram
- "Topping off" of a seller's prepaid credit or debit card
- Online payment methods not listed above

This policy not only applies to what you have listed online but to any correspondence between the buyer and seller. In addition, a seller cannot add any surcharges onto the price of the item, such as for acceptance of checks, money orders, electronic transfers, or credit cards.

Link Policies

You can have links off your listing, as long as they follow the policies of eBay. Here is a list of types of links that are not permitted. Follow this policy, as failure to do so could cost you your PowerSeller status and membership on eBay.

- Links that lead to Web sites or pages that offer to trade, sell, or purchase goods or services outside of eBay.
- Links that lead to sites that solicit eBay User IDs, passwords, or e-mail addresses from buyers.
- Links that encourage buyers to place their eBay bids through a site other than eBay.
- Links that lead to live chat systems.
- Links to videos hosted on other Web sites.
- Links that lead to a place to subscribe to newsletters or mailing lists hosted outside of eBay. As a business, you can follow up later with opt-in newsletters, but you cannot place this link on your auction page.

Titles of Listings

Do not use titles that are misleading in order to bring buyers to your listing. Here are some eBay rules to follow when creating a listing:

- The title or subtitle must accurately describe the item for sale. It cannot contain false or misleading information.
- You cannot list an item in a category that is not representative of the item being sold.

- You cannot use brand, product, or celebrity names inappropriately throughout a listing. An example is comparing an item to another brand named item's style or connecting a celebrity indirectly to the item being sold.

- There cannot be information in the description that contradicts any of the options selected through the Sell Your Item page.

CHAPTER 3

Communication is the Key

Tips from the Experts

Here are some of the major obstacles I had to overcome:

- *Knowing what quantities to list for maximum margin.*
- *Knowing what times to have the auctions close.*
- *Knowing competitor pricing on items to know what to sell and what not to sell.*
- *Building a customer base to increase the feedback rating; this will actually make people pay more for an item through you.*

— Michael Jordan, Owner of Bullystick Direct

Offering high-quality products at low prices is not enough. You have to let people know you are out there. The Internet is expanding at an exponential rate, and it is easy for your online store to get lost amid the hundreds of other online stores offering similar products. An online business that does not have some sort of an online marketing strategy is doomed to fail. If no one knows you exist, then no one will come buy your wares.

When used correctly, e-mail can be a powerful tool. It can bring the message of your business to your target market. Despite all the SPAM and other junk mail out there, you can create e-mail that is dynamic and useful to your growing business.

You have to let existing customers know that you still have products to offer them. An e-mail campaign is critical to retaining existing customers while seeking out new ones. It is a good way to interact directly with potential customers. Many of the consumers who come to your online store do so via products you have posted on eBay. Without a solid strategy of creating repeat customers, you will have one-time customers who will only use eBay for future products rather than seeking your business out specifically.

For instance, Jake is engaged to Fiona. When Fiona was a child, she loved Mickey Mouse. Jake wants to get her something special, so he gets the idea in his head to go and buy her a Mickey Mouse collectible PEZ dispenser. Jake logs onto eBay and immediately stumbles upon the link to your product, because you currently have in stock a whole crate of collectible Mickey Mouse PEZ dispensers. You have the best price, the best photo, a nice description of your product, and a terrific seller record, which makes Jake trust you. Jake buys the PEZ dispenser for his fiancée. She loves the little mouse that dispenses candy, and his purchase was a success. This could be the end of the story, if you let it.

Jake does not know that you offer many other things at unbelievable prices. You specialize in all types of PEZ dispensers and other collectible toys. Jake loves collectible plastic toys. The sure-fire way to get Jake to come back and use your eBay store again is through a successful use of e-mail so that you can clue Jake in to the wonderful promotions you are having for all sorts of wonderful products.

You must carefully consider your e-mail options. Knowing how to and how not to use e-mail is vital to a good customer/seller relationship with customers like Jake. The proper or improper use of e-mail can mean the difference between Jake being a lifelong customer or a customer you will never see again. If you do not create the e-mail in the correct manner, it could end up in his SPAM filter, and he may never read about your fantastic offerings.

Opt-in E-mail

Nothing is as annoying as, or less profitable than, SPAM. Most people will not read it, and you will be wasting valuable time and money sending it out. Savvy Internet users have SPAM filters that enable them to avoid SPAM altogether. If you send out unsolicited e-mail and alert a SPAM filter, it can end up in the trash quickly.

It does not cost anything to add links to your eBay store, an "About Me" page, or a personal Web site in an e-mail. Use the signature section (an option you need to use and fill out in your e-mail provider's setup) to place this information in every e-mail for you so you do not have to retype or copy/paste the links all the time.

Start saving your customers' e-mail addresses right away. Use your address lists to announce new products or other big news from your business. You do not want to bombard your customers with e-mails, as you may then be relegated to their "blocked senders" lists, but you do not want them to forget you, either. Seasonal e-mails can be a happy medium.

For every season, e-mail your customer list with a new announcement, product promotion, and a wish for their happiness in the months to come until you e-mail them again. Express your sincere desire to do business with them again.

You must make sure that you respect and record "opt-out" messages. All businesses must be sensitive to customers who do not wish to receive e-mail, so keep your own list of those who contact you and wish to opt out. You should also include a statement about what you do with your collected customer e-mail addresses. Let customers know that you value their business and have no intentions of ever selling, renting, or trading e-mail addresses with anybody else.

If you are looking for a way to supplement your own customer database, you can purchase e-mail address lists that are generated from "opt-in" clauses on Web sites. These tend to be more reputable sources of e-mail addresses than some other lists you can buy, but beware that you still may be regarded as SPAM by the recipients. Make clear in your e-mail title that you are not SPAM. Many companies also offer to actually do the e-mailing for you, using opt-in lists they have on file. There are scam artists posing as reputable marketing companies who simply send SPAM with your company name attached to it. Tread carefully when contracting with any other company to do the e-mailing for you.

For the most part, at least for now, obtain your e-mail list from your own customer base, and guard it carefully. Your customers will thank you for protecting their privacy and not adding to the SPAM in their inbox every day.

Creating Your Own List

Do not be sneaky about getting people to sign up for your e-mail lists. Nothing is more annoying than buying a product from an online vendor, and then suddenly having your mailbox overrun with junk mail. I recently bought something on eBay from a major retailer; not five minutes after I purchased their product, I had about ten e-mails from them that I did not ask for. I went to their site and checked some of the e-mails for an opt-out policy and found that there was no opt-out policy. Annoyed, the only thing I could do was to block them from my e-mail account, since they kept filling up my inbox with e-mails I did not want. Do not make this mistake. You will lose repeat customers, and even worse, you will damage your reputation. The single greatest — and free — marketing tool is word of mouth. If you damage your reputation, you will destroy this powerful tool. People will not recommend your company because SPAM makes you look amateurish and desperate.

Do not send customers e-mails too often. A monthly update e-mail is a good way to keep customers connected to what you are offering that they might want. Keep the e-mail short, and use proper English and grammar. If you are unsure of your writing skills, hire a writer to do e-mails for you.

You can find many solid freelance writers at reasonable rates on sites such as **www.Elance.com** and **www.Guru.com**.

Reread every e-mail several times before you send it, and take an objective look at what you are sending your customers. Your customers will appreciate your attention and respect. Repeat e-mails or poorly written form letters are indicative of an amateur, and this is not the road to becoming a PowerSeller.

Having an opt-in policy allows your customers to decide whether they want to receive e-mails from your online store. You can use eBay's tools to include an opt-in invite whenever you send out any correspondence. Every customer interaction is an opportunity to add to your list, even if the customer is only asking questions about your products.

If your eBay business is coupled with a physical storefront, you can ask visitors who come to your store to sign up to opt in as well. Also, if you visit trade shows or sell your merchandise at some other venue, make sure you have a clipboard handy with a sign-up sheet. You might be surprised how many people are willing to give their e-mail addresses out if they like what they see.

When creating your list, you can use various incentives, such as discounts on your products, product giveaways, sales, coupons, and other advantages to make signing up for your e-mail list appealing. For instance, Borders Books and Barnes and Noble both have online stores, and both send weekly e-mails with discounts and coupons if you join their members program and opt in for their e-mails. You can learn from these big companies, as the same benefits can apply to your small business. You can form an incentive program for your e-mail campaign that will have people waiting to receive your e-mails and promotions.

Using a Third-Party Mailing List

Many third-party companies out there compile opt-in lists for sale, yet you must use caution when purchasing such a list. Although there are many legitimate third-party companies out there who offer real incentives to the people who sign up for their services, there are also many companies that are doing this unethically. Do your research and find out how the company obtains their information, and how useful that information is.

These third-party companies are like shopper clubs that offer their clients discounts, free products, cash back, and other incentives to allow them to sell their contact information to vendors who they think match their interests. To join an incentive club, you may have to complete a survey that lists all your interests and all the categories of vendors that you would not mind contacting you. For instance, on the survey, there might be a box to check if you enjoy hiking and the outdoors. If you have an online store that deals with hiking gear and outdoor activities, the third-party company would compile a list of every person who checked that box, and then they would sell you that list. This can be a powerful tool, especially when you are just starting out. Imagine suddenly having a list of potential customers who you know will like the products that you have to sell.

Find out how they target the customers who are on their lists. Only those companies that do their homework, including specific research into the interests and hobbies of their clients, will have lists that are of any value. Companies that solicit members with an ad like, "Click here to receive some special offers from our friends, and receive a free gift!" will be worthless, and could cost you a fortune. Also, find out how frequently those lists are sold and used; an overused list will be worthless, as well, as the customers' mailboxes will be so full of unwanted junk mail that yours will get lost in the slush pile.

Newsletters and HTMLs

Any e-mails that are just lists of things you are currently offering are not likely to be read, and they may not help draw customers back to your online store. One solution is to offer some type of newsletter and spice it up with some simple hypertext mark-up language (HTML) graphics. Although you do not want to go overboard with all the glitz, eBay has some relatively simple-to-use seller tools that will allow you to add things like pictures, backgrounds, fonts, and graphics that will make your newsletters look professional and sharp.

Newsletters can also be an excellent place to offer free advice and information about the specialty niche marketplace, if you have a target audience. For instance, let's suppose you sell video games all over the world; you could send out a newsletter giving free advice about gaming, the latest system reviews, and other things that would matter to die-hard gamers. Looking at the types of games you sell the most should give you some idea of what types of articles will get read, and what will lead people to see you as an authority in the marketplace.

For instance, let's say your highest selling type of games are role-playing games (RPGs) like World of Warcraft (WoW); articles that will most likely be read will feature information relevant to customers who prefer to play RPGs. Then, you can include in your newsletters those items that any serious gamer would love to have. They will go to read the articles and see that you are offering something that they have wanted to buy at an unbelievable price. Top it off with some good coupons that are sure to get their attention, and your newsletter just generated a sale.

Newsletters can be monthly, biannual, or yearly in frequency, or you can just use a standard one you send out to explain who you are and what you sell. They can contain facts about your particular business and some interesting facts about the items you are selling.

If you have a regular newsletter, you can focus on different aspects as they correlate to products you offer and how they are used. You can send these newsletters to potential or new clients. The information contained should be helpful and should give suggestions of other items you have to offer that they may not have seen when buying from your online store. It is important when you are discussing an aspect of your items that you include a link to them on eBay so readers can start bidding right away.

If you want to tackle creating a dynamic newsletter, here is a list of desktop publishing programs and their average prices at the time of this publication:

- Art Explosion Publisher Pro: $90
- Page Plus: $30
- Print Shop Pro Publisher: $95
- Microsoft Publisher: $99
- Print Shop: $45
- Print Shop Essentials: $15
- Publishing Studio: $100
- Design & Print: $40
- Print Workshop: $20

More expensive does not mean better. Print it on good stock paper and use a decent printer if you are mailing it out. Otherwise, have it printed by a professional, such as Kinko's. You need to consider the cost of printer ink, paper, and your time when making your decision. You can save the costs of mailing them by sending them via e-mail.

Try to keep your newsletter to two to four pages. You can use the front and back to save money on paper and postage. Make it bright and eye-catching, and make your information easy to find.

If you are not a writer, or do not have time to write, there are many freelance writers out there willing to do all the research and writing for you for a modest fee. Web sites like Elance.com are places where freelance writers have organized so that people looking for content know where to go to find high-quality writers. Also, Guru.com is an excellent place where people looking to employ writers can post what they are looking for, and then the freelance writers will bid for their business.

As eBay has a limit to how many e-mails you can send a month, hiring freelancers for a modest cost is a solid way to make your online storefront look amazing. If you hire a professional to do the writing, you will likely be pleasantly surprised with the results. The more research you expect them to do for you, the higher the price tag will likely be. If you have some research done for them, and merely need them to write 500 words about it, the price should be much more modest.

If you choose not to hire a professional writer, be aware that grammar counts. Do not be sloppy. Do not use slang or Internet speech, like lol, rofl, or any other shorthand spellings. Keep all your e-mails grammatically correct, professional, and friendly.

Also, make sure your e-mail address is professional. Although clever e-mail addresses might have been cool in college, they most likely will not inspire confidence in your business among your customers. Stick to something professional, like a combination of your last name and some numbers or the name of your company. Many Internet service providers now have free e-mail services, and they will often let you have as many e-mail addresses as you want.

Tips from the Experts

Five-star customer service; quick shipping; great communication; unusual, hard-to-find products; international buyers; and willingness to answer any question from my customer about the products I sell are my company's greatest assets.

— Charlene Anderson

Programs that Manage E-mails for You

There are many programs available for sale that can significantly increase the speed and accuracy of your e-mail campaign. This enables you to send mass e-mails effortlessly, and it can even be set to automatically send e-mails that you pre-write. For instance, you can have automatic e-mails sent that thank your customers for doing business with you, let them know that their package has been delivered, remind them to give feedback, or invite them to join your mailing list. All you have to do is write the template — or in some cases, select a template from a previously generated list — and the program will do things like enter the customer's name and other relevant information.

Nonetheless, most people find that the built-in eBay stores' e-mail marketing program is satisfactory for all their needs. If you decide to invest in a commercial program, make sure that it has functions that are not available to you already free via eBay. The number one mistake of many people who are just starting out in eBay is rushing to buy all sorts of fancy programs and gizmos without first realizing how many powerful tools are already built into their eBay seller account. Get to know your eBay store, and you may find that what you need has already been provided.

Below is a brief summary of what to do and not to do:

Do...

- Include useful information in your e-mails, such as informative articles and tips
- Include an "opt-out" with your e-mails so recipients can opt not to receive your e-mail promotions
- Include an "opt-in" with your orders so your customers can opt to receive your e-mail promotions
- Give recipients of your e-mails something "extra," such as a special price or discount

Do Not...

- Buy bulk mailing lists
- Send out e-mail promotions too often; once a month is enough
- Include attachments in your e-mails; people will suspect that they are Trojan programs and will not open them
- Post self-promoting entries to newsgroups or forums

Tips from the Experts

I use Vendio to manage my auctions, inventory, and photos and Endicia for shipping (anyone who doesn't use this in an eBay business is crazy). I flag e-mails that need to be attended to, my iPhone substitutes as my brain, and a Levenger Circa notebook is always in my purse or by my computer for all the things that need to be on paper.

— Charlene Anderson

Tips from the Experts

To be honest, I outsource a lot of the "work" to others. I'm a big believer in keeping my time as free as possible while others sweat the small stuff. I'm also not a big fan of selling hundreds of items at a time on eBay. It's too risky to have all your eggs in the eBay basket.

I practice and teach multiple income stream strategies, and I keep them all as "autopilot" as possible. For managing my eBay account, I use eBay's own "Selling Manager Pro," and it's worked great for me.

The automation feature is great because on some of my information products (I sell those on CD), I can set the eBay listing up so that whenever the listing expires, or the product gets bought, another listing appears automatically without me even logging in to eBay. What's even better is that I have a third party service set up to professionally package and ship out the orders as they come in. I never touch that part of my business!

My advice is to always be outsourcing and automating every possible aspect of your business. Your time is far too valuable to ever get bogged down doing what I call "$10 per hour" work.

— Jim Cockrum

Seller Tools

Many tools can be found under **pages.eBay.com/sell/tools/list/** on eBay. Some of these tools are free, and some cost a few dollars. Many new sellers do not know they exist, while others are using them every day. You may not want to buy or use all these applications, but they are worth looking at and considering. As they are specifically created for eBay sellers, they are user friendly and are easily integrated into the eBay system.

Let's look at a few of the seller tools available to you through eBay.

Sell Your Item (SYI)

The Sell Your Item (SYI) is a tool that allows you to quickly list your items. You can create customized listings and tool guides easily through the listing process. The SYI form offers you time-saving features. SYI allows you to keep a draft of the form you did not finish creating; you can go back and work on it later. The form allows you to remove steps and customize your form with colors, fonts, and reusable templates. SYI also allows you to receive more categories to look over for your items.

Turbo Lister

One of the best things about this tool is that it is free. This tool can help you create professional listings and allows you to upload them in bulk sets. It has search tools that allow you to find items quickly. It also boasts a dynamic toolbar that allows you to control your listings more efficiently.

This tool was created with the PowerSeller in mind. It allows you to create your listing offline and then upload multiple listings all at once, which saves time and aggravation. You can also duplicate and copy existing listings to create new listings of your inventory.

My eBay

This tool is already integrated and free. You should look this tool over carefully and see whether you are using it to its maximum potential. My eBay allows you to see all your selling activity in one place. You can see what listings are active and what their starting dates were. You can also easily view what the current prices and bids are on your items and manage cross promotions from this area.

You can add notes to help you keep track of items you are selling; you can also use picture manager under this tool to manage and view all the pictures on your listings. There are status icons with the listings that allow you to keep track of which items have been paid for and shipped, and you can manage your feedback on your items. This area allows you to see your selling reminders. These are important to keep track of so that you do not miss an auction that has ended or needs attention.

Selling Manager

If you want to go to the next level of managing your listings, you might want to consider trying this utility. This tool is free for 30 days, and then you can continue to use it for $4.99 a month, or, if you are a Basic Store subscriber, it is free. Selling Manager works with Turbo Lister and allows you to monitor multiple listings and give bulk feedback, which can save you time and money. You can also print invoices and labels in bulk for your shipping needs, and it will automatically relist items as you sell them. There are e-mail templates and feedback responses stored in this tool.

Seller Dashboard

Another free feature that sellers sometimes neglect to use and monitor is the seller dashboard. It is available to view after you have ten or more DSRs. On this board, you can view your most recent 30-day DSR scores. You should use this feedback to improve and tweak your eBay business. Bear in mind that it is repeat customers and word of mouth that create true PowerSellers. You can easily compare your scores with the average eBay seller. You can also review what the minimum requirements are for rewards. It is here that you see what it takes to achieve PowerSeller levels and fee discounts.

On this dashboard, you can see what your current standing is in search results. This can help you maximize the visibility of your listings when they are sorted by the Best Match feature. This tool also shows you how eBay views your ability to deliver your items and connects this to your eligibility for incentives or risk of penalties. You can see whether you have violations and learn how to avoid restrictions.

Finally, you can view your balance, payment status, and other related alerts. Look at this dashboard daily, as it can help you increase your sales and status, and can even save you money in discounts.

Selling Manager Pro

As this book is for the advanced user, you may be ready for more advanced tools. If you have outgrown the Selling Manager, you may be ready to use the Selling Manager Pro. You can try it out for free for 30 days. After that, it could cost you $15.99 a month, or it is free if you have a subscription to Premium or Anchor Store memberships.

This tool helps by having a full sales-management function. This allows you to create and even schedule your listings in bulk batches. This way, the listings are placed on eBay at certain times without you having to do anything further. It contains a designer utility that allows you to create more professional listings. As listings are posted, it automatically decreases or increases your inventory.

Selling Manager Pro can save you time by automatically sending feedback when you receive a payment from a buyer and then sending them an e-mail when their item is shipped. A more advanced feature that you might be interested in is the ability to create monthly profit and loss reports. These can work easily into the business plan you are creating. To determine whether you have the right price set on a recurring item, you can see a particular product's success ratio and the average price it is selling for. A nice function of this utility is that you can export your sales data to QuickBooks using Accounting Assistant.

Blackthorne Basic

This tool, free for the first 30 days and $9.99 a month thereafter, allows you to create and edit bulk listings. It contains a number of easy-to-use templates. This tool will insert payment terms, shipping information, and other items automatically into your listings. There are a few bulk-listing utilities, such as sending bulk e-mails and feedback to buyers, and it will also mark the status of payment and shipping in bulk batches.

Blackthorne Basic saves sales and customer information for later retrieval. It also has a number of different invoice templates.

Tips from the Experts

I use eBay's Sales Manager Pro to keep track of orders and listings. I use Blackthorne Pro for listing. I automate wherever possible. Routine customer e-mail and feedback functions can all be automated.

— Tom Orr

Blackthorne Pro

This utility, free for 30 days and $24.95 a month thereafter, was created for high-volume sellers. It contains the features of Blackthorne Basic with a few more exciting tools.

This Pro version contains free listing templates and client-controlled listing schedules and will increase or decrease your inventory automatically. It can also create listings that are linked to other items you are selling.

The more advanced features include bulk printing of labels and invoices, the ability to create monthly profit and loss reports and support multiple user profiles so different people within your company can access information, and the ability to manage your suppliers and consignment clients.

File Exchange

This tool is available for free to qualified sellers. The qualifications are that you must have been on eBay for 90 days and averaged 50 or more listings a month for the past two months.

This utility allows you to edit a listing or update the status of a listing and leave feedback all in one file. You can download your active listings and sales reports in a flat file format. You can then import this file into your own offline software for manipulation. This utility can create a template for any category you wish.

The nice component of this utility is that it allows you to create listings from any software application you choose. It even supports Internet Web-page posts.

Now that you are aware of the powerful tools you might need as an advanced seller on eBay, you must decide which one is right for you. Fortunately, eBay has two ways in which they can help you chose.

You can go to **http://pages.eBay.com/sell/toolrecommendations.html**. On this page, you just choose how large your company is and what types of features you want, and this utility will make recommendations for you.

Or you can compare the different tools side by side at **http://pages.eBay.com/sell/toolrecommendations.html**. This shows the different features available with each tool to help you make a decision. You should try some of these tools out. You will be amazed how much easier some functions, such as mass listings, can be.

Tips from the Experts

I try to be organized in all of the aspects, and I have a visual "how to" book that I have put together for anyone that needs to fall into my shoes should I be traveling and shipments need to be made. I use a Blackberry to follow sales and make plans on when to schedule the day for shipments. If I see that an international sale came through, and I am away, I immediately contact the office at home to pull the item and give me a weight. I then use the notebook computer to log on to eBay, PayPal, and FedEx sites and send the packing slips, customs forms, and customs invoice and shipping label to a PDF file. I then e-mail that file back to the home office so the shipper can just print the PDF and ship. I guess in short, I have found a way to run the business from anywhere, as long as I have help at home.

— Jimmy Stewart

CHAPTER 4

The Auction

Before there was eBay, there were live auctions. These auctions are accentuated with a number of people with identifying cards that they hold up when they bid. There is an auctioneer who moderates each item up for auction. They show the item, describe it and its history, and begin with a starting bid. People hold up their card to indicate that they were bidding. Bidding eventually stops, and the one with the highest bid wins the item with the slam of a gavel. There was a time when eBay had live auctions, but for many reasons, it did not work out as well as live auctions do in specialized auction houses.

I am going to take you through each step of the auction process to offer you tips to save you money and time and to attract more buyers.

Placing Your Auction on eBay

There are many tips throughout this book for placing your item up for bidding. There are many things to consider, such as adding on extras to your auction to make it more attractive. The important thing to remember is that you need to cover your costs while setting a bid that does not scare off potential buyers. If you cannot place an auction that at least covers your costs, then you should not list it. You should be striving to make a profit, even if it is a dollar or two on each item. If your listing is costing too much, cut out some of the extras. If you have to set your price too high, you will not only not sell the item, but you will be out the insertion fee and any extras you bought to list the item.

Look at how other people's items that are similar to yours are selling. Some products are seasonal, and it may not be the right time of the year to sell them. Some of the items are fads that have flooded the market, and no one is interested anymore. If you have many items that will not sell, consider selling them as a lot. This will save you individual listing costs, and it will be more attractive to buyers, as they will be getting more for their money. This is a good way to move old merchandise.

Start the Bidding

You must start with a price that is attractive to buyers. The magic of eBay is that as the bidding goes up, people will often pay more for an item than they intended to. This is to your advantage. You must start with the right price to get the ball rolling. You must cover your costs and you must make a profit. Make it interesting, but do not think that your buyers are not wise to the starting price of 99 cents for the newest electronic gadget. They will know that there has been a reserve set. Just set reasonable prices, and people will come and buy your items.

At the level of PowerSeller, it is about bulk. Do not get hung up on making hundreds of dollars on one on or two items. You must look at the large picture of how multiple auctions will make you hundreds of dollars. Even if you do not get as much as you wanted on a couple of items, do not be discouraged. You are building your reputation and your number of sales for PowerSeller eligibility.

Timing

In the world of eBay, timing is crucial. There are good times and bad times to sell, and good auction lengths and bad auction lengths. Ask any PowerSeller when the price goes up on an item and they will tell you that this happens during the last half-hour of an auction. Why people have auctions that are drawn out for weeks depends on the item. Hot items will have bids coming in during the entire duration, while items that are flooding the eBay market will sit quiet until the end.

If you have a hot item that is going fast, you can set your bidding for one day. People will bid fast and hard to get the item. The good thing is that if you are using just a one-day auction, your listing goes to the top of the results list. If you choose the one-day format, consider having your Buy It Now price at least 50 cents below your competition's, and consider making your starting bid a few dollars below your Buy It Now Price.

If you are looking for a slightly longer auction, consider the three-day format. This works well with items that will shoot up in price quickly after posting. Three-day formats work well during the holidays for last-minute shoppers. If you see that a week-long auction is going well, consider putting up a three-day auction during the last few days with a similar item. Your buyers will jump over to the new item and immediately begin bidding on that one because the price will be lower.

The next duration is a five-day auction. These work well during holiday rush time or if you want an extended weekend.

The seven-day auction allows more time for people to notice your auction. This gives people more time to find and bid on your item. These auctions work well for bulk sellers. This gives you at least one weekend, which is a good shopping time, but is not so long where people are not interested anymore.

The ten-day auction costs an extra 40 cents for auction-type listings but is free for fixed-price auctions. This length of auction can give you two weekends if you time it right. Ten-day auctions are good for rare and expensive items.

The ending time is important for an auction. The timing of the auction is exactly one, three, five, seven, or ten days to the minute of when you place the listing. Late at night is not the best time to post a listing, as it could end at 2:00 a.m. The best bids are during the last part of most auctions. You can set a specific time for the listing to post as an additional option.

The best time for ending auctions is something you can research. Look at your past auctions and see what you bestselling-times are. This depends on what you are selling and who is buying many of your items. Selling many items overseas can have an impact on the ideal time and date of your listings. Here are the best days, in rank order, for ending auctions:

1. Sunday
2. Monday
3. Thursday
4. Tuesday
5. Wednesday
6. Saturday
7. Friday

This is based upon PowerSellers' input and can be different for your individual business, but this is a good place to start. There are days that you should not have items end on, as they are the days when prices drop the most; these include the Fourth of July, Memorial Day, Labor Day, and Veteran's day.

Repeat Business

Repeat business is like money in the bank. If you have regular customers, you will be able to spend less time and money attracting new ones. Making a buyer happy also increases your feedback scores, which helps you gain and maintain your PowerSeller status. Word-of-mouth advertising is golden. Below is a list of tips to show that you will go the extra mile to gain and maintain a customer. Anyone can sell a doll on eBay, but only a PowerSeller who is on top of customer service can grow a company. eBay is not just a fancy flea market online.

- If you are selling used equipment, take the time to clean it up. Make sure it is as clean and new-looking as possible. It is important for the merchandise to look its best when it arrives with the customer.

- You can entice a buyer to look at your other items if you have them clearly listed and connected to your auctions. You will get quicker results. Make sure you have a number of Buy It Now items to choose from.

- Include buyers' positive feedback when listing similar items for future auctions.

- If there are any kind of flaws or damages on an item, make sure that you not only list it on your auction but that you provide close-up shots of it for the buyers to view. That way, when they receive the item, there are no surprises.

- When selling items like cars, make sure you list everything you can about them, including flaws or scratches. Customers are relying on your honesty to buy an item sight unseen, so do not hide anything. It will only hurt your reputation.

- Make sure that your buyers can get a hold of you. If they see your contract information available, even if it just an e-mail address, they will be more confident buying from you, and they can get a hold of you after the sale if they need to. You may even find that buyers will contact with praise or questions about other items you have for sale.

- When you mail the item, include a sales slip, invoice, and copy of the listing. You may even put a small note or a catalog in if you like. Never send the item without documentation included.

- Provide as many payment options as possible. Not everyone is computer savvy, so be patient when they want to send a check. Wait until the check is cleared before sending an item. Do not be scammed.

- You can learn from the mistakes of your competition. Look at their negative feedback to find out ways to improve your customer service and avoid pitfalls.

- Never delay shipping an item if possible. Make sure it arrives while they are still excited about the item.

- Try to send a little extra. It can be a document explaining the item, or some other similar object of small value. Even small extras will get your buyers to notice and remember you. It costs little to make people happy. Consider sending older inventory that has not sold.

- If you have similar items, consider offering a Second Chance Offer to the losing bidder. It will save you on the costs of creating a new auction.

- Offer a return policy for items at the seller's shipping expense. Allow customers to change things like size or color. You might make an extra sale in the process.

- When creating a listing, create bullet-point summaries of items that have a large description. Make the summary highlight the main exciting points.

- Create a scale to describe items' condition and post this with your auctions. Rate each item's condition on that scale so that the buyers know exactly what they are buying.

- When posting new items, consider posting them at the same time every week. That way, your buyers will know when to look for your new merchandise.

- Create a Frequently Asked Questions (FAQ) link on your auctions and Web site. Include all of your policies, such as shipping costs and returns.

- When you get a used item, look for descriptions, and keep a database of what the item looks like and functions like when it is brand new. This way, when you post an auction, you will be able to compare your item to the new item.

- Offer your buyers discounts on future items or same-day purchase items through your store.

- Do not forget that the worth of an item is only as high as a bidder is willing to pay for it.

- Do not use cutesy listing titles. All titles must include the description of what you are selling.

- Always strive to look and act professional. When you use several exclamation points, or try other tactics of making the words look unusual, you will look like an amateur. Use the tools at your disposal to increase your sales, not gimmicks.

Relisting

Sometimes items will sell like hot cakes, while at other times, you could hardly give them away for free. This is the nature of selling on eBay. Changing trends and reaching the wrong customers are often the two things that can throw a wrench into moving slow merchandise.

Here are some tips to follow when considering relisting items:

- If an item is hot and sold with some heavy bidding, make sure you list a similar item quickly. You may want to even list it before your original listing ends. If someone did not win a bid or a bid goes too high, they will be looking for a similar item quickly.

- When listing a similar item, choose the "Sell Similar" option.

- When relisting an item that has not sold, choose the "Relist" option. This is important because you will be able to recoup your listing fees if it sells the second time. You can only do this twice. On the third time, it will be listed as a Sell Similar item, but will not offer a refund of fees. On the fourth round, you will be able to recoup your fees again.

- When relisting, you need to think through your title, category, and listing price. Do research and see how other people are selling similar items.

- Remember that even eBay is run by supply and demand. If eBay is flooded with an item, the price will go down, but if you cannot keep an item in stock, the price will go up.

- Consider using Second Chance offers to under-bidders to move similar merchandise.

PowerSelling Tip

Sell items as a collection or set rather than one piece at a time. They will sell faster and gain more interest.

CHAPTER 5

Lowering Shipping Costs

Tips from the Experts

Charge a little higher price on an item that doesn't cost that much to ship, and then offer free shipping. People love free shipping, and then they have to give you a good rating on your shipping charges.

— Michael Jordan

Tips from the Experts

Always ask for discounts. Look for ways to automate. I found a shipping program that costs me $24 per month but cut my shipping time in half. The shipping process used to take nearly half a day. Now it takes less than two hours.

— Tom Orr

Getting Paid First

The first thing on your to-do list is choosing how to receive payments. Do not wait until after you have posted an auction to think about these things, as items may sell quickly, leaving you with a buyer waiting to pay and no idea how you want that done. If you put something such as "payment and shipping to be determined by the end of the auction" in your item description, people will know you are new, and they are hesitant to do business with people who simply do not know what they are doing. Bear in mind that at this stage, you are trying to become a PowerSeller, so you need to look as professional as possible.

There are numerous ways you can receive payments from your buyers, and each has its pros and cons. Being aware of all the options can help you make an informed decision that will lead to your company's policy on payments. How you accept payment is up to you, but it is wise to maintain the same policy, regardless of the auction item.

The six basic ways to receive payment are cash, personal checks, money orders, cashier's checks, escrow services, and PayPal.

Cash may seem like a logical choice, but few sellers will accept this payment type, even though they can avoid any PayPal fees and other nuisances, such as check-clearing time, by doing so. For one thing, if the seller never receives the money, the buyer may not believe it and might accuse the seller of receiving it and not shipping the product. It is too risky a venture, and not worth the hassle. When sellers do accept cash, often you will see this notice in their payment policy: "Cash at your own risk."

Personal checks are another payment form not commonly accepted on eBay. When sellers do accept them, they commonly have a disclaimer in their payment terms stating that they will hold merchandise for ten days to assure that the personal check has cleared. Most buyers accept this requirement.

The good thing about having a buyer send you a personal check is that, as with cash, you avoid any fees from electronic transfers. For the buyer, it is cheaper and easier than going out of their way to purchase a money order or certified check. However, for many power and high-end sellers, this option may be too time consuming to track.

A better option to personal checks is accepting money orders and certified (bank) checks. Money orders are less secure than bank checks, but both are still considered more secure than personal checks. Most sellers do not hold off shipping until these items clear.

PowerSelling Tip

There have been many reports of counterfeit Postal Service money orders in the past few years. The Federal Deposit Insurance Corporation (FDIC) Web site has a special bulletin about counterfeit money orders and how to determine whether a Postal Service money order is authentic. See ***www.fdic.gov/news/news/SpecialAlert/2005/sa2305.html*** *for this bulletin.*

There are numerous companies that sell money orders, so to protect yourself, a good policy is to ship all items after your bank has accepted the money order for deposit. Your bank will be happy to examine any money orders for you. It saves you and them time and aggravation should the money order be returned.

If you do want to accept checks, then cashier's checks are normally considered an incredibly safe form of payment, although most people do not want to pay the extra fees for them unless you demand it. If you are selling an expensive item, consider asking for only electronic payments, such as PayPal or a cashier's check. It is always possible that even this type of check can be counterfeited, especially if it is from a bank on the other side of the country that you have never heard of. The best way to make sure is to ask your bank to look at it.

Another way to secure payment for those expensive or rare items is by using an escrow service. An escrow service is a third party who receives the money from the buyer and holds it while the seller, knowing that his or her money is secured, ships the product. When the buyer has had a chance to inspect the purchased item, he notifies the escrow service to release the funds to the seller. There are fees involved, and the process can take time, but eBay recommends using an escrow service if the auction price is over $500. Search eBay's Help Directory for "escrow" to see a list of suggested escrow companies and read more about the process, fees, and terms.

The final and most commonly used payment option is the electronic payment company, PayPal. This system performs most of their functions directly through the Internet. PayPal, found at www.paypal.com, works by obtaining funds from the buyer's bank account, credit card, or debit card. Buyers can choose the funding source(s) they wish to use. Although this can cause some major headaches for sellers, it is worth learning how PayPal works and its policies. The good news is that PayPal and eBay are liked, so payment is a smooth process that does not require signing off one service and opening another. Even shipping can be done through PayPal.

PayPal has changed their policies and offers in the past year or so. You can now use PayPal for your eBay transactions without having to upgrade to a new level of membership. They offer extra tools to make the connection between eBay and PayPal seamless. They offer shipping and tracking options and will automatically send this information to your eBay account. When you use this service, it will ask whether you agree to connect your accounts, but it is worth the time and effort and is relatively simple.

There is a catch: PayPal will deduct a commission before depositing the money into your PayPal account. For sellers who have $3,000 or less coming into their account every month, that fee is a flat 2.9 percent + 30 cents for each transaction. The 2.9 percent is taken from the entire amount of money transferred to you from the buyer — including any shipping and handling charges and sales tax you collect. If you are selling an item for over $3,000, the percentage deducted is much less.

Monthly Sales Price per Transaction

Amount Sold per Month	Fees you owe to eBay
$0.00 USD - $3,000.00 USD	2.9 percent + $0.30 USD (per transaction)
$3,000.01 USD - $10,000.00 USD	2.5 percent + $0.30 USD (per transaction)
$10,000.01 USD - $100,000.00 USD	2.2 percent + $0.30 USD (per transaction)
> $100,000.00 USD	1.9 percent + $0.30 USD (per transaction)

PowerSelling Tip

If you have a buyer bidding on multiple items from you, ask them to hold off paying until all the auctions they are bidding on have ended. Then, they can pay all at once, and you will only be charged the 30 cent transaction fee once.

If you want to have the funds in your PayPal account transferred to your bank account, there is no charge, but the process could take several days. This makes it almost easier to purchase postage and business supplies through retailers who accept PayPal payments. PayPal does offer a newer service of a credit or debit card. You must apply for the credit card, but the debit card is free and works much the same as your bank debit card. You are given a PIN number and can access funds that are in your PayPal account instantly.

PowerSelling Tip

If you display the PayPal logo in your listings and state that you accept PayPal payments, you cannot state in your listing that PayPal payments made via credit card will not be accepted. This policy can be found at this link: ***http://pages.eBay.com/help/policies/seller-non-performance.html****.*

Having a PayPal account is essential when running an eBay business, especially if you wish to be a PowerSeller. Trying to manage and direct buyers to different accounts all the time will not only add to the chaos, but will add to your record keeping and accounting tasks as well.

If you wish to sell items from your Web site, you may wish to consider Web site Payments Standard or Web site Payments Pro.

Web Site Payments Standard

- Works with all major online shopping carts
- Includes "Buy Now" buttons
- Allows you to accept donations
- Allows to you use gift certificates to make purchases
- Allows for subscriptions and recurring payments
- Includes Virtual Terminal, which allows you to accept phone and fax payments
- Allows your buyers to sign up for PayPal
- Allows you to create custom checkout pages for a consistent look

- Allows you to accept multiple currencies
- Provides a record of your PayPal transactions and the ability to download your logs into programs such as QuickBooks
- Provides a log of monthly credits and debits on your account
- Allows for advanced search for transactions
- Includes the ability to refund customers
- Includes integrated shipping services
- Includes a sales-tax calculator
- Includes fraud and chargeback protection
- Provides instant payment notification
- Allows you to withdraw funds with your PayPal debit card
- Includes a “Mass Pay” option
- Allows you to send money to and request money from anyone with an e-mail account

Web Site Payments Pro

The Pro version contains all the standard features, in addition to the following:

- PayPal Shopping Cart
- Auto Return feature to bring buyers back to your Web site after they pay
- Encrypted Web site Payments
- Payment data notification
- Web Services and the ability to build new applications on your site

The standard version of Web site Payments is free, and the Pro version costs $30 a month to use.

Brief Explanation of PayPal Features

PayPal logo and taglines: PayPal can add these automatically, or you can insert a set of logos manually. Go to the "Auction Tools" tab in your account for detailed instructions on setting up either of these options.

End-of-auction e-mail to winning bidder: This is a nice service because even if you are not online to see your auction ending, PayPal will notify the winning bidder, and then, if you have already set up your shipping options properly, the bidder can pay immediately via PayPal if he or she wishes. This slick feature benefits PayPal too; with PayPal being the first in line to accept payment, buyers do not have to think of choosing one of the other options.

History log: The history log lists every transaction for the previous three months sorted by date. To access it, click on the "History" tab in your account. You can select from several different options for searching the history from searching by transaction type to searching by date.

Downloadable log: This is an excellent way to speed along your record keeping. Download this log monthly and keep it with your monthly sales ledger. Backing up your data in your sales and inventory ledgers is always wise.

Monthly statement: Sign up to get a monthly statement by going to the "Profile" tab and clicking "Link," then go to the site to print it monthly; new statements become available on the 15th of each month. Keep these just as you would keep your monthly bank statements. Reconcile them by comparing the totals with your ledger, and if there is any discrepancy, you can compare your downloaded log transaction by transaction.

PowerSelling Tip

PayPal statements are only available for three months back, so if you forget to print one, do not wait too long or it may be gone.

Refunds and fee credits: If you need to make a refund to the buyer, go to the specific transaction. If it is not listed on the "My Account" tab page, then click the link at the bottom of that box that says "All Activity." This takes you to a screen where you can pull up information from the past three months. You can make refunds for up to 60 days after the transaction first took place. Simply click on the transaction you wish to see, and click the refund button. PayPal will walk you through the rest of the necessary steps.

If you refund the buyer's entire payment to you, PayPal will refund you the fees they charged. They do not offer a refund of fees if you only make a partial refund to a buyer.

Buyer and Seller Protection provided by PayPal: Thoroughly read all the information on PayPal's Web site about Buyer and Seller Protections, as the information here is just a snapshot of the programs. You will find detailed discussions about these features under the "Auction Tools" tab when you are logged in to your account.

Buyer Protection is available with all account types, but in order for the buyer to be protected, the seller must have done certain things first.

Some of these requirements include:

- Your eBay feedback score must be at least 5.0 with 98 percent or better positive feedback
- You must be a verified member of PayPal
- You must be a seller in one of twenty listed countries; the United States and Canada are included
- Your account must be in good standing
- You must have the "Buyer Protection" icon displayed in your Seller Information box on eBay
- You must use a shipping service that allows you to track the shipment, in case of a claim that the item was never received

Buyers also have requirements they must meet, including time limits; they must make their claim within 45 days of the PayPal payment. The buyer also must have paid using the seller's e-mail address, as stated in the listing.

A buyer might file a claim if they never receive the item or, as PayPal's Web site terms it, if the item is "significantly not as described." Merely being less than thrilled is not an excuse for filing a claim. Buyers are limited in the number of claims they can make per year as well. Of course, buyers and sellers are always encouraged to work things out themselves first without resorting to filing claims, which should always be a last resort.

PayPal cares about the sellers they serve, as well. They offer a Seller Protection plan that helps prevent fraud. They work hard to prevent fraudulent chargebacks and will also help you fight a chargeback if you have sufficient documentation to prove that the chargeback is not necessary. Sometimes, PayPal can respond quicker to resolve a situation than eBay can.

Some tips that PayPal offers to help you defend yourself include the following:

- Use tracking tools with every shipment. These can include delivery confirmation, which is required for every shipment when you purchase postage through PayPal; insurance; and actual "tracking" (if you use UPS, FedEx, or other carriers).

- Ship to the buyer's confirmed address only. Be suspicious of buyers who want their items sent to different addresses, especially in different countries. In the transaction details, it will say "Confirmed" after the address.

- Check buyers' eBay feedback for a broad view of their reputation.

- Check to see whether the buyer's PayPal account is verified, which means that his or her bank account has been confirmed by PayPal.

You can check the status of a buyer right from the transaction page. Simply click on the link for Details. Look for this:

Payment From: Seller's Name (the sender of this payment is Verified).

All users should become familiar with the "Profile" tab on their account pages. Here, you can manage every detail of your account and even see what other services or features you may not be using, such as creating custom templates for invoices. It is worth spending a little time clicking all the links just to learn about how PayPal can work for you.

With over 78 million accounts, PayPal is by far the largest online payment company. And because it is an eBay company, it is quite easy to use with eBay. It is available in 45 countries and in 6 different currencies. Plan on accepting PayPal for most of your payments. Get to know all the options, and use all the tools available to you. If you make it work for you, your account fees will be well spent.

Getting a handle on payment choices is a large task, and one you should have under control before you start your first auction. Trying to scramble and set things up after the fact will not help you project a professional image.

Tips from the Experts

I was purchasing shipping supplies from a local office supply store (one of the big three), and one day, I stumbled upon a wholesale packing supply house that would sell directly to me. I was able to cut my waterproof bubble packing envelopes for the books and media by 80 percent, and the customers love them because it keeps the books dry and still protects them. The other thing is that using Endicia and Ship Rush software for shipping allows me to integrate right into the eBay Selling Manager by pulling the seller name, address, e-mail, and item information right into the label. All I need to do is input weight and print the label. The confirmation or tracking number is then automatically sent to eBay Selling Manager and to the seller. So the buyer knows the item has been shipped and when to expect it, along with tracking information. This all saves time and cost.

— Jim Stewart

Refund Policy

There are plenty of eBay sellers who state prominently in their "About Me" page and on each listing, "All Sales Final!" This is an overly strict policy that will not win you any friends and will discourage some people from bidding at all. If a customer has never bought anything from you, he or she does not know you at all, has never met you, and is considering buying a product based only on a description and photograph, not having actually seen it in person. You are just a page on the Internet, and customers have plenty of reason to be distrustful.

Of course, you have no intention of being dishonest, but you have to communicate that to your bidders through friendly policies. You will not get that many returns (unless you are selling substandard goods), so you do not have much to worry about. Every physical store in the world builds a certain number of returns into their pricing structure. It is inevitable that once in a while, something may get broken in shipping, or when it arrives, it may not be what the buyer expected. Instead of imposing a strict "No Returns" policy, create something a little friendlier. Create a return and refund policy stating that you will graciously accept returns within a set time — for example, 30 days. Be sure to state clearly in that policy how shipping fees will be handled and what you expect your customer to do to facilitate the return and refund.

Fulfillment Options

Fulfillment is what a person who shops in an actual physical store gets to experience right away. For instance, Patty is from Peru, and she has lived in the United States for about ten years. One day, she is walking through the mall, and in one of her favorite clothing stores, she sees a t-shirt that says, "Peruvians Are Awesome!" and it is her favorite color, hot pink. She is overjoyed, and even though she was not expecting to spend the $24.95, she does. As soon as she pays for the shirt and it is in her hands, she is experiencing fulfillment. Fulfillment is the gratification a customer feels immediately after a sale is complete.

Fulfillment can be thought of as exactly as it sounds: the fulfillment of a sale. It is the conclusion to the act of buying that leaves the consumer feeling satisfied and content. This is the major advantage brick-and-mortar stores have over online stores: instant fulfillment. If you are going to be successful with your online store, you are going to have to consider your fulfillment strategy.

One of the major reasons that online stores fail on eBay is lack of an idea of how they are going to complete customer fulfillment. Just go to eBay and find a seller who has a high profile rating, scroll down the list of customer comments, and you are almost guaranteed to see that at least most of those positive comments having something to do with the customer receiving the merchandise in a timely fashion. Your customers are not stupid; they choose their shipping methods carefully, and after they purchase that item on your online store, they count down the days until their item comes. If you can pleasantly surprise your customers by getting the item to arrive much sooner than expected, you are almost guaranteed to get some positive feedback.

High profile ratings are important to customers, and they will likely not buy from a seller whom they do not think they can trust to bring the online transaction to a satisfactory fulfillment. Follow these basic guidelines to make sure you are bringing all your transactions to their proper fulfillment.

Fulfillment 101

- Do not charge for time, gas, and/or miles used going back to the post office. That will drive your prices up because you will have to charge more for shipping, and most customers have some idea how much it should cost to ship whatever it is they have bought. Only charge what it costs to ship the item.

- Reuse shipping materials. When you buy things to resell, or you receive inventory, make sure you hold onto that shipping material so that you can reuse it. This will lead to significant savings in shipping costs.

- Buy shipping materials in bulk. The cost of a shipping container may not seem like much, but if you are shipping items every day, you will save significantly if you buy in bulk. Go to your local Office Depot or Staples and buy all your envelopes, bubble wrap, and packing tape in bulk.

- Be honest and up-front about how much it is going to cost to ship something. Do not surprise the customer with "hidden shipping fees" at the end. As they already want the item, they may still buy it, but they will not be happy with you. Do not forget that if you get too many complaints about excessive shipping costs, eBay could shut you down.

Tips from the Experts

I needed a way to store the inventory in a small dense location but still be easy to get to it. Ship the items out in a reasonable time. My shipping goal is to ship within 24 hours, and I really try for 12 hours (excluding weekends and holidays). The inventory obstacle was resolved by installing wire rack shelves in the basement. I use the 52-quart clear storage tubs from Wal-mart and have an eBay label on the front of each starting from tub # 1. I use the hidden comment area in the eBay item listing to indicate where the item is located and the price I paid for it. For example, comment "1.00 63" means I paid $1 for the item and it is in tub number 63. I stack the books so I can read the spine from the outside thru the clear plastic. I use this same method for small parts and other items.

— Jim Stewart

Keeping Track of Your Inventory

Have a system to keep track of inventory. In the last chapter, I listed some tools that eBay offers that can help keep track of your inventory for a reasonable price. You can also choose to use a Microsoft Excel spreadsheet if you are familiar with this program. You can find plenty of books or even take a course at a local community college to hone your Excel skills. You need to have a good system for inventory, because you want to be sure that you have the item that the customer is looking for and know where it is so you can send it right away.

Where you are going to store your inventory is a decision that must be carefully thought out. For a modest fee, you can store your merchandise in an outside warehouse, or, if you have the room, you can choose to store items in your garage or basement. Having your inventory at home means that you do not have to pay anyone to hold or store your items, and you do not have to pick up your merchandise somewhere else before shipping. Everything is right there in case a customer has a question about an item.

You might also need to consider heat and humidity. Some items may not be affected by temperature and moisture, but others can be destroyed. You must consider what types of items you have and decide on the best place to store them. Mold can also destroy items such as books or other paper products.

Wherever you decide to store your items, make sure that they are away from water. Sometimes, basements can flood, which could destroy an entire inventory. Check for rodents and bugs as well. Keep the area exterminated, as pests can also destroy hundreds or thousands of dollars in inventory.

Be careful of stacking items, as things could get crushed or broken. Spread out your items so that you have easy access to them and they will not topple as you are pulling an item to be shipped.

Ship Right Away

Even though it may seem pointless to make a trip to the post office to ship a small, $1 item that a customer just bought, it will mean something to your customer. Get into the habit of making this trip at least once a day, especially when a customer has placed an order. Try to consolidate your trip as much as possible, but do not delay shipping for days just because you only have a few items to send. Shipping is just as important as any other eBay business function.

It may seem like it is a better use of your time to wait until you have several items ready to go out or to do it once a week or so; resist the temptation to do this. Your customers take the recommended shipping times quite seriously. If it says two to four days, by day five, they are getting a bit upset. Make them wait a week, and you are almost sure to get a nasty comment, a negative feedback rating, and a customer who will not buy anything from you ever again. Set a time each day that is your post office time, when you will drop off any merchandise that is ready to be shipped. Do this every day, and use e-mail to let them know when their product has been shipped.

There are a number of stores, such as Mailboxes Etc., that will ship from different shipping services such as the Postal service and UPS. Find one in your community, and you can cut your travelling down significantly.

Scheduling Regular Pickups

Once you have a high volume of outgoing products, you can save plenty of time by printing out your own postage on your computer and scheduling regular pickups of outgoing mail. As long as you have an account with a post office, FedEx, or UPS, they will come to your home and pick up boxes.

I will encourage you throughout this book to access services offered through eBay. There is no sense in starting from scratch when eBay wants you to succeed. When you succeed and are making money, they are also making money. They want to help you in any way possible to sell more products efficiently, and for the best prices possible. Repeat customers for you also mean repeat customers for them.

If you have not done so, go to eBay's shipping center. If you follow the instructions found here, you will be able to estimate your shipping, print out shipping labels, and even track your shipments; they also have tips on shipping. You can even order shipping boxes for free that have the eBay logo printed on them from United States Postal Service (USPS).

Should I...

...buy sellers insurance?

Insurance is meant to protect the seller, as they will be held responsible for products that have been damaged or were lost during shipment. Things rarely get lost, so you can save money by only insuring products that could potentially break during shipping or that are expensive to begin with. You can save a small fortune in insurance fees if you only insure items that you are genuinely concerned about being damaged. It is your responsibility if something gets broken, not the buyer's. This point can be argued, as they can also buy insurance, but if the product is faulty, it is your business that will pay in the long run with bad feedback and lost customers. If an item is returned, then you are also losing money because you have paid for shipping and eBay fees for an item you may not be able to resell.

...outsource my shipping?

A fulfillment center is an organization that specializes in sending out other companies' products. They have their own warehouse and trained staff who will make sure all your products get to where they need to go quickly and efficiently. If you have a high volume of outgoing goods, outsourcing your shipping may be a good idea for you. Many higher-volume eBay PowerSellers have found that outsourcing their shipping has saved them time and money. If you are thinking about hiring a fulfillment center to store, pack, and ship your goods, then you might want to consider whether you have enough outgoing products to make outsourcing your shipping cost effective. Based on the outsourcing options available to you, is it going to cost you less to ship through an outside agency based on the rates for their services? If it is, then you should outsource.

Outsourcing may not work if you are selling unique items. If you have the type of business dealing in, say, antiques, and your inventory will be changing all the time, outsourcing will not be practical. It would cost you extra just to send the items to the fulfillment center. On the other hand, if you are selling bulk lots of PEZ dispensers, then a fulfillment center may be a better option.

Pros to Outsourcing Shipping:

- **Lower Cost**. Since fulfillment centers deal in extremely high volumes, they are able to pack and ship for much less than it would cost you. They take buying in bulk to a whole new level. Instead of buying a carton of envelopes, they are able to buy envelopes by the truckload, which significantly lowers their overall costs.

- **Less Work**. They will run the warehouse for you, and you will not have to deal with renting a warehouse or other real estate to store and pack your goods. The major advantage to this is that it allows you to work from home, even after your product volume has expanded beyond what your home can handle.

- **Organization**. They have advanced inventory systems, with bar codes and everything, which will enable them to ship things much more quickly and accurately than you would be able to.

- **Regular Reports**. Most fulfillment businesses give their clients regular reports on the status of their products. This takes care of the business of keeping track for you. All you need to do is put all the reports they send you into a three-ring binder or file folder. No more filling out pages in a notebook or spreadsheet.

Tips from the Experts

In all the years I've been selling on eBay, the only shipping supply I've had to buy is tape! I ship green! And to help with the acceptance of my used shipping products, I created a site called: ***http://GreenShippingRocks.com****. I write this on all the plastic bags or used envelopes in big bold letters. Then, when the customer receives the item, they can see the pledge I've taken to "Ship Green." I've gotten connections at Doctor Offices for great packaging supplies. I advise my students to find a local source and set up a plan for picking up the bubble wrap, popcorn, foam boxes, or whatever their needs are. Pediatricians and hair dressers get tons of items with mint packaging supplies ready for recycling!*

— Danna Crawford

Methods of Shipping

Unless you are outsourcing your shipping, you only have three real options: The United States Postal Service (USPS), The United Parcel Service (UPS), and Federal Express (FedEx). Each offers various incentives for choosing them as your shipping service, and we will examine each in depth.

PowerSelling Tip

Pay attention to how long it takes you to process and ship an item. Look for ways to reduce the amount of time and make the process more efficient.

Shipping with USPS

Pros

- A preferred shipping provider of eBay, they have a variety of tools fully integrated into the buying and selling of online goods.

- It is integrated into eBay's shipping calculator and PayPal, which allows potential customers to determine whether they should buy something from you or whether it would be cheaper to drive to a store and pick up something equivalent.

- You can purchase your own postage through the USPS Web site or PayPal and print it out on your home computer.

- You can purchase insurance and get delivery confirmation straight from your PayPal account.

- Priority Mail comes with no additional fees besides the cost of postage and insurance.

- Delivery confirmation is free for Priority mail and is only 13 cents for other mail classes.

- Their Web site offers a "Calculate Postage" link so you can calculate the estimated postage for the customer, so that they do not have to look it up.

- Free co-branded (both eBay and USPS logos) boxes for Priority and Express mail classes that come in three different sizes.

- Two sizes of flat-rate boxes, meaning the price is the same regardless of destination or weight for Priority and Express mail.

- All these boxes are available free to sellers, but only for Priority and Express mail, and only for auction items.

- When you purchase your postage through PayPal, you have the option of scheduling a regular pick-up time from your local post office, which can help immensely if you do not live close to the post office, or if you are going to be away from your home or office and still want your products to be picked up.

- For rainy days, you can even get a covered plastic container and make arrangements for the carrier to take your packages out of that instead of stacking them by the mailbox.

Cons

- For other mail classes besides Priority and Express, you have to purchase all your own packing materials.

- Insurance and delivery confirmation is just your receipt to prove that you did actually ship it. If the customer claims they did not receive the package, you have no way of knowing whether they received it. Also, you will not know whether the customer received the item in question until they leave feedback. If they do not leave feedback, you can only assume that as long as they do not complain, then all is well.

- Only Express mail allows for a version of package tracking. For all other mail classes, a signature confirmation or return receipt is only available for a price, and if you are particular about managing the details of your customer fulfillment, this can get expensive.

PowerSelling Tip

Look for ways to sell to international buyers, but be very careful about fraud — especially in underdeveloped and African countries.

Shipping with UPS

Pros

- They have an extremely user-friendly Web site with tools for small business owners. You can go to their Web site and look at all the ways that they want to make your life easier.
- They will store your customers' addresses online for you if you like, which, if you have plenty of repeat customers, will significantly increase your productivity.
- Their tracking tools for business owners are better than the USPS tracking system.
- You can easily arrange for pickup right on their Web site.
- You can create up to 20 shipping labels on their site.
- You get e-mail notifications of all your deliveries so that you do not have to keep tracking them.
- They are better than USPS for shipping large, bulky items.

Cons

- You need to supply your own shipping materials.
- They are not quite as integrated as USPS.

Shipping with FedEx

Pros

- They have the most user-friendly of the three Web sites, with excellent drop-down menus that will direct you to all your shipping needs.
- They offer various incentives for switching over to them.
- You can get an account with them, which has a variety of positives, such as the ability to choose to be billed for all your shipping needs once a month instead of every time you ship something, which immensely simplifies things.

Cons

- The only cons with FedEx are the same as the cons for UPS.

To cut costs and maximize profit, your best bet is to determine which shipping company will offer you the best rates for each of your shipping needs.

CHAPTER 6

Seller Beware: The Importance of Protecting Yourself

For as long as people have bought and sold goods, some have sought to obtain money through dishonest and fraudulent means. The Internet is no different; it has its share of crooks who, given the opportunity, will take your money, and may even try to steal your identity.

These thieves can be anywhere. You can be operating your business out of a small town in Montana, while someone in the Ukraine is trying to hack into your system to get at your PayPal and bank account password. There are a host of other frauds and scams that the online business owner must contend with.

This chapter is meant to help you deal with this reality of e-commerce. Now, even big companies understand that there will be a certain amount of loss each year. What they ask themselves, and what you should be asking yourself, is how much loss is an acceptable loss, and what steps should be taken to deal with this loss.

There are certain steps that you should take to prevent it from happening, but you should expect a certain amount of a decreasing rate on your returns. Even most security experts will accept this as just a part of business.

As a business owner, you must decide what steps are necessary to protect yourself, and what should be treated as an acceptable loss.

Ways to Protect Yourself

Secure Your Passwords

Memorized passwords are one of the easiest ways hackers can get into your computer and cause real, lasting harm. If you use the same password for everything, or if you have an easy-to-recall password, it can be either guessed or, with patience on the part of the hacker, a brute force program can try hundreds of different passwords in an instant, eventually unlocking bank accounts, PayPal accounts, or even your eBay account.

With passwords, live by the following rules, or you are leaving yourself wide open to a possibly traumatic theft. This type of identity theft is becoming so common that most banks, credit cards, and other money managing corporations will hold you responsible for fraudulent charges or deductions. They have reasoned that people leaving themselves open to hackers in this way is no longer an acceptable loss. Since the perpetrator can be anywhere in the world, these "identity thieves" are rarely caught.

Password Security Guidelines:

1. **Change your password regularly, for instance, about once a month**. Some security experts will counsel you to change your password even more often, about once a week or so. As long as you are consistently changing your password, you should have no problems.

2. **Never write down your password anywhere, as you never know who might try to cause you harm**. Do not trust anyone. Neighbors, friends, and others who traffic your house may snoop around in your stuff and steal your password. On hacker discussion boards, the most reliable, easiest way of hacking a person's password is by gaining their trust and then stealing their password by either having the "victim" tell them the password or by looking into their records when they are not around. This is called "social hacking."

3. **Always use a mix of alpha and numeric characters**. Some passwords have become so common that hackers use them first, like "password," "letmein," "123456," your name, the name of your spouse or other loved ones, or a pet's name.

4. **Your password should be at least eight characters or longer,** since as you increase the number of characters in your passwords, the number of permutations a brute force program must perform to crack your password becomes almost infinite.

Get a Good Firewall

In homes that are built side by side, or in apartment buildings, separating one room from another is something called a firewall. A firewall is a wall that is built extra thick and of more expensive, flame-retardant material than other walls so that a fire in one home or apartment will have a harder time spreading to another.

A firewall for your computer is something that protects your computer from the unwanted invasion of foreign parties. If your computer does not have a firewall, it is like a city without any walls, and it is vulnerable to invaders who are then able to just walk right in and take whatever they want.

A firewall does not need to be the most expensive thing you buy for your online business. Computer companies specialize in making these firewalls effective and relatively inexpensive. It works like an invisible wall around your computer by keeping out unwanted intrusions into your computer that can either harm it or allow someone from outside access to sensitive areas.

Use a URL Filter

Many Web pages contain "active code" in their Web addresses, or Universal Resource Locators (URLs), which means that as soon a page is open, programs start running. Some of these are innocent, but many of these will try to install some type of "malware" (software that will harm your computer), such as spyware, adware, Trojan programs, and others that can do serious harm to your program by either directly harming your computer or by stealing vital information stored in your computer.

Get a good URL filter and a good spyware blocker to help protect yourself from attacks against your computer.

Different security tools you need to have on your computer:

1. Anti-virus service
2. Anti-spyware
3. Anti SPAM
4. Firewall
5. URL filtering

Keep everything up to date. Pay attention to when their subscriptions run out, and renew with the companies that provide the software as needed. Also, check often for updates that may be available for these programs. In most cases, you can set them up to automatically update so you do not have to do anything.

Protecting Yourself from Fraud

Scams from Suppliers

As the owner of an eBay business, one of your chief concerns is finding product to sell. Thieves know this, and they will try to use it to their advantage. Most legitimate sellers know the reality of illegitimate suppliers' scams, and they will try everything to put potential customers at rest. Be on the lookout, use some common sense, think before you buy, and follow these basic guidelines:

- Do not believe the hype of "get-rich-quick" schemes or outrageous claims of high profits.
- Only buy from suppliers that have actual physical addresses.
- Do not buy supplier lists. More often than not, they are useless, and you can often get the same information online by doing a little research.
- Stay far away from multi-level or pyramid marketing schemes.
- Try to only buy from a supplier with a proven track record and a list of references.
- There should be a support call number or a help desk that answers all your questions in a helpful, respectful manner.
- If you are going to be buying a large supply of these products, they should be willing to send you a sample product for free or for a small fee.

PowerSelling Tip

There are many different scams related to eBay. eBay will never send you an e-mail requesting any identifying information, password, bank information, or any personal information. These are scams. Delete them, and do not go to any links provided. If you have any questions, go directly to the site and send an e-mail to customer service. If you want information about current eBay frauds, go to ***http://pages.eBay.com/securitycenter/avoiding_fraud.html****.*

Delivery Confirmation

Many dishonest buyers will order products by standard USPS shipping because they know that USPS does not track these packages, and the seller would have to pay extra for delivery confirmation. When the package arrives, they will file a complaint with eBay or PayPal that they did not receive their item. If you do not have proof that they received that item, you will have to send another one or they can refuse to pay you. When they refuse payment, unless you have paid the extra 50 cents or so for the delivery confirmation, which is just a receipt saying that your package was indeed delivered, you are out of luck. Now that dishonest customer has a perfectly good item that they can use or resell for an extremely marked-up price, since they did not pay anything for it at all. This is the online equivalent of shoplifting.

Many sellers calculate the extra 50 cents into their budgets for the added peace of mind, and if you are an online customer, you should receive an e-mail from the USPS when your parcel reaches its destination. Some sellers are so worried about this type of fraud that they refuse to ship via standard mail. The mistake there is that many honest customers do not mind waiting the extra time it takes the item to travel to them via snail mail, as long as they are getting the lowest possible shipping rates. Honest, good customers that you want may not buy from you because you will not offer them the type of low shipping costs they want.

You must think about what is an acceptable amount of loss regarding steps you take to avoid getting scammed. If you only ship parcels with shipping methods that you can be sure will give you accurate delivery confirmation and tracking, then most likely, you will not be scammed, but you may lose significant business.

Phishing

Phishing in the real world is where a man dressed in some sort of official capacity strolls into an office with a clipboard and a work order. He gets signed in by the receptionist, and then proceeds to snoop around the entire office. Let's say he was pretending to be a computer technician; he might even try to steal several computers. And since everyone in the office thinks he must be there for a reason, no one stops him. In the full sight of everyone, he will make out with possibly thousands of dollars worth of equipment, not to mention the sensitive company files he may have gotten his hands on.

For the online environment, let's use an example of phishing. You are working on your computer, when suddenly a window pops up from PayPal stating that they need to make sure that you are the real user of this account. There may even be some official-sounding warning on the page about phishing scams. The page may even look identical to the login screen that appears when you first sign into PayPal. They will likely ask you to verify your identity by inputting your username and password.

Do not do it. Do not click on any link in that window. Although the aforementioned Internet security programs minimize such intrusions, it is hard to stop all of them, and at some point in your life, you will encounter these; this recently happened with MySpace. A hacker or a group of hackers managed to replicate the MySpace sign-in page. After people sign in, they frequently surf other people's sites as well. At some point, they press the back button on their browser, and then they find themselves back at the sign-in page. Thinking that they must have accidentally signed out, they re-input their sign-in information, and then the hacker has all their account information to do with their personal Web sites whatever they wish. By and large, they would use the hijacked sites covertly, not changing their login information, but using the site to advertise to everyone on their friend list by posting bulletins or leaving comments about such and such an offer.

If you ever have any doubt about the integrity of the page, contact the page's owner immediately. Most services that require you to sign in state that no one from their company will ever ask you for your username and password.

Shielding

Another tactic that an unscrupulous buyer may try is called shielding. They will have another user bid incredibly high, which will cause other buyers to back out, but then, at the last minute, that high bidder will back out as well. This acts like a shield, deflecting the other customers and allowing another to come in and win the auction at the lowest possible price.

They only way to protect yourself against this type of fraud is to keep track of these bad customers. Pay attention to user ratings, block users with bad user ratings from your auctions, and try to avoid selling to customers with poor ratings. Unfortunately, that is the only way you can protect yourself from such dishonest individuals.

Identity Theft

If you find that you are unable to log into your own account suddenly, you may be the victim of identity theft. Here, someone has gained access to your account and is pretending to be you. They may then be running auctions as you or buying things with your money. Contact eBay and Pay-

Pal immediately to try to rectify the situation. Then, look around eBay to see whether you notice any activity bearing your name that you did not conduct.

Liability Insurance

You may have grown accustomed to having certain things, such as a house, a car, and savings. If so, you should be aware that you could lose it all. You need liability insurance, which covers you and your business. The type of insurance you get and the type of business structure you are working under will determine how much personal liability you are covered for. You should ask an insurance agent. Try to find an agency that works specifically with online businesses or even eBay businesses. You can ask other eBay business owners whom they would recommend.

One of the things you should consider for your business is liability insurance. There are different types of liability insurance depending on the types of products you are selling on eBay. Business liability insurance covers you in case of any lawsuits concerning property damage or personal injury. The products you sell on eBay could injure someone and you could be responsible for any injury, not eBay. You could lose not only your business but your personal property could also be in jeopardy. You may have asked yourself how can you afford insurance. If you are moving to the level of PowerSeller, you will be moving with the big dogs. You cannot afford not to protect yourself, because you will have more to lose.

Types of Business Liability Insurance

- **General Liability Insurance**: I would recommend this type of liability insurance for most PowerSellers. Its policy usually covers injury claims, property damages, and advertising claims. This type of insurance also is known as Commercial General Liability (CGL). For most PowerSellers this is all the liability coverage they may need, so it is a good place to start.

- **Professional Liability Insurance**: As a PowerSeller, you should never need this type of coverage, because this usually applies to those professionals providing a service of some kind like a doctor, lawyer or counselor. I list it here solely to inform you of its existence so you will be less confused when you are shopping for liability insurance.

- **Product Liability Insurance**: Since you are providing products, you may need this type of insurance. If you are creating a product like a dog treat, you are responsible for any damage or injury it could cause. There are different levels of this type of insurance depending on the level of risk your product can pose to the general public.

When shopping for liability insurance you can contact your local Chamber of Commerce or other similar trade organizations. Sometimes they offer good deals for their members and policies that are specific to the type of business you are running or for the type of products you are selling. You can find listings of different agencies that offer liability insurance on the internet or certain trade magazines. You can look in the back of many of these types of magazines in their classified advertisement sections.

Take the time and compare the rates and coverage from a few different companies before settling on a particular policy. The research and time you invest could save you hundreds of dollars a year. When comparing coverage look for things such as whether they cover legal fees, and how much of those fees they will cover.

To gain a better perspective of the amount of coverage your eBay business needs, look at eBay company lawsuits online. See how much companies have had to pay out. Ask around and see what other companies are covered for.

Sometimes you can land a package deal with a company if you are buying more than one policy or you already have other insurance policies in place. You can decide whether a package deal of policies is the best fir for your growing business. You do not need to be covered for everything under the sun, but you need a minimum amount of coverage for the more common situations you could find yourself in. It seems that everyone is suing everyone. You may not want to advertise that you have liability insurance, because some unsavory characters will target you as a company that they could potentially get a decent payout from.

Choosing a Business Structure

You need to also consider what type of business structure you have. If you are starting a business with you as the sole owner, you would file a Doing Business As (DBA). This is the process of securing the name of your business. You must understand that if you file as a sole proprietor, you are liable for losses, bankruptcy claims, legal actions, and more. As you are personally liable for these things, you could lose personal and business assets.

Business Name

You cannot just use any name. Some names are trademarked. There may also be some state regulations that may prohibit some specific words from being used in your company name. You should check for state regulations concerning naming a business. You can go to **www.uspto.gov** to see whether your name has been trademarked. You can also do a Google search of the name and see what comes up. This will especially be important when choosing a domain name for a Web site.

When you choose a name, you may want to register and trademark it. You will register it as a DBA, which will allow your company to exist as a separate entity from you. If you choose a Limited Liability Corporation (LLC) structure, the process of naming your business will be a much more official process. It is necessary for an LLC to come up with a unique name that is not currently being used by any other LLC, and it must include the letters "LLC" or its equivalent at the end of the company name. Owners of an LLC will then reserve their company's name at the Secretary of State's office in the state in which the business is run.

If a corporation has been chosen as a preferred business structure, the process of naming the business comes with even more formalities. Like LLCs, corporations must reserve their preferred business name with the Secretary of State's office in the state in which their corporation is run. They must also include "corporation," "incorporated," "Corp," or "Inc." somewhere in their business name at the end so that the public will know the business is a corporation.

Another thing to consider, in terms of naming a business, is whether you will need to trademark your business name. The U.S. Patent and Trademark Office defines a trademark as being "any word, name, symbol, or device, or any combination, used, or intended to be used, in commerce to identify and distinguish the goods of one manufacturer or seller from goods manufactured or sold by others, and to indicate the source of the goods." Although you do not have to register to trademark a business, there are a number of benefits if you do, including easier registration for dealing with foreign countries, nationwide recognition of your company, and ownership of a trademarked name. To register for a trademark, you will need to contact the Trademark Electronic Application System (TEAS), which can be found online at **www.uspto.gov/teas/index.html**. The form can be filed at the Secretary of State's office, or through the U.S. Patent and Trademark Office for more protection.

Although there are many benefits to trade marking, a smaller business not planning on working with foreign countries, or on a large scale, will have less need for a trademark.

Since the business is conducted solely online under eBay, the Small Business Administration (SBA) suggests registering a business name as a domain name. Unlike business names and trademarks, domain names are registered online under various online businesses.

These businesses will require a search to make sure a name is not taken, which will require a small fee. If you choose this option, you will have the advantage of having your business more publicly recognized because it is both a dot-com and an actual business.

You must still make sure that your business name is not taken on the domain level, as it cannot be used twice. It is important for you to put plenty of thought into your business's name. A name that is too corny or serious will give customers the wrong impression. A business's name should convey, or at least hint, at what type of services the business will provide to the public. A business will be looked to more quickly if the name offers what customers need. A business's name should be straightforward; too many clever names just get lost in the shuffle. After you come up with a good name, and go through the proper steps of acquiring that name, you are ready to begin forming your chosen business structure. Some structures are easier to form than others — namely, sole proprietorships, partnerships, and LLCs — but it is still important to go through every motion, no matter the size, to ensure a successful formation. Corporations require significantly more paperwork and licenses. Following is a sample statement for a DBA:

Statement of Intention to Conduct Business under an Assumed or Fictitious Name

The undersigned party does hereby state his/her intention to carry on the business of ________________________ , at the business location of _________________________, in the City of _____________________ , in the State of _____________________ ,under the assumed or fictitious name of: ____

The owner's name, home address, and percentage of ownership of the above-named business are as follows:

Name:
Address:
Percentage of Ownership: 100 percent

Signed on _____________________ , 20___

____
Business Owner Signature

____
Business Owner Printed Name

In addition to a DBA, you may choose to trademark your name. It is up to you whether this is necessary for your particular business. If you are interesting in trade marking your name, you can find the necessary forms and information at **www.uspto.gov/**.

If you intend to have a partnership, you may have a few of options. You can form a general partnership, which is less involved than if you tried to form a corporation. Each partner would be responsible for what the other does, so it would not hurt to have an attorney draw up some partnership papers. They do not have to be legally filed, but it will help with possible problems and misunderstandings in the future.

LLC

If you are sure you have found the right person to form a business with, you might consider an LLC. An LLC creates a tax structure of a partnership, but also protects the owners from personal liability, thus protecting the owners' personal assets. Forming an LLC requires more effort than forming a sole proprietorship or partnership, but less than forming a corporation. The first thing that must be done is to file "articles of organization." These articles are more like certification, sometimes known as "certificates of organization," and are filed through individual state governments. The fees for filing these articles are between $100 and $800, which is still less costly than forming a corporation. Depending on the state in which a business was formed, these articles can be one page or several.

Most states only require the address of the business, the name of the business, and the name of a resident agent, which is also required for filing for a corporation. After filing the articles of organization, an LLC "operating agreement" must be written. This agreement is not filed with the state, but rather in the company being started. It sets the guidelines for the members of an LLC, including the responsibilities of its members, members' interest percentages in the business, and the members' shares of the profits of the business. This agreement states how much money members of the LLC will get and what their job description will be. After this agreement is written, some states will require an LLC to publish a "notice of intent," which simply states your intent to start an LLC and is published in a local newspaper.

Finally, to form an LLC, you will have to get the proper licenses and permits to operate your business. The permits and licenses required vary from state to state, but include a business license; an employer identification number; a zoning permit, if the business is in an office building; and a seller's permit, depending on what goods are being sold.

It is also important to make sure that limited liability is included when starting an LLC. Some states require you to pay extra for this, and it may end up being less costly to start a corporation. Without limited liability, an LLC is nothing more than a sole proprietorship with more acting members. You should also consider getting good business insurance that includes a liability policy.

Corporation

The other type of legal arrangement that can be considered with a partner is a corporation. This goes a step beyond an LLC in that it creates a separate entity from the owners. It is an involved process that includes filing articles of corporation, electing officers, and holding an annual meeting. For many smaller businesses, this may be more trouble than it is worth. In addition, a corporation must pay corporate taxes, which can be cost-prohibitive for many small business owners. There are benefits to a corporation, such as the ability to obtain financing much easier than you can alone, which can help if you decide to expand or franchise your business.

If you decide to go the route of becoming a corporation, you may consider hiring an attorney. While it may save you money initially to file it yourself, it could cost you later due to the complexities of corporate law. If you do decide to navigate the process of creating a corporation, a description of the process follows.

The first step for registering a corporation is incorporation, and it is almost always completed on the state level. This process simply involves choosing a name for a corporation in accordance with the state's rules in which the business was formed, and the amount of paperwork varies from state to state. Since this step makes up such a large chunk of the registration process, it is imperative for you to know everything about the state government in which the business is formed.

After incorporation, all other licenses and permits must be acquired from the state and federal governments. The required licenses and permits are different for everyone and depend on the state of formation and the market type, although federal documents are required of everyone.

After all the paperwork has been completed, it is time for the corporation to organize the structure of its new business. You will need to appoint directors to all necessary positions in the corporation and create corporate bylaws, which spell out the rules that must be followed to operate the corporation.

Since corporations are required to have a board of directors, those individuals will be required to hold a meeting and note official minutes for the corporation's files. The final step will require the owners of the corporation, also known as shareholders, to issue all stock in the corporation.

State Requirements

Much of registering a corporation is done through the state government in which the corporation was formed, forcing the business owner to decide what state the business will be registered in. Many states have strict requirements of corporations, while others are much more flexible. Some business owners will choose to form their corporation in a different state than where it will be operating. These businesses are called "foreign corporations" and require additional procedures to be allowed to operate. It is important to know the advantages and disadvantages of each state and the terms for forming a business in a different state before deciding which state the paperwork will be filed in. If your business chooses to conduct business in more than one state, you will have to file the proper paperwork in each state individually. This option can get expensive and time consuming, but can pay off with the amount of income being acquired. Some people choose to form their company in certain states because of the leniency or flexibility they offer.

Incorporation

For a corporation to be created, it must go through various steps outlined by a process called "incorporation." This process is the act of a new business registering with the government, and it requires a pile of paperwork called "articles of incorporation." The articles of incorporation are fact sheets for the government to keep on file that have any information regarding a new corporation. To incorporate a new business correctly, you must acquire all necessary licenses and permits and file paperwork with various organizations on the local and national levels.

Incorporation was originally required to prove to the government that the corporation was started to serve some type of purpose, and incorporation allowed individuals to spell out their business's purpose more easily. In time, though, incorporation became a valuable resource for corporation owners to make more money because it allowed for a clear separation between them and their investors.

Information Needed for Incorporation

- Name of business
- Selection of legal designator (e.g., Inc., Corp., Co., Company, Incorporated, or Corporation)
- Physical address of business
- Purpose of business
- County and state where business is formed
- List of other states in which business is located
- Start and end dates of business's financial year

- Name and address of resident agent
- Type of corporation (C or S)
- Names and addresses of any heads of the business (including president, secretary, and treasurer)
- Names and addresses of company's directors and shareholders, if applicable (for shareholders only: List the number of shares owned and assets they contribute)
- Description of share type business will use

Following is a helpful list of information to have handy that the majority of states require in filing for incorporation:

State Taxes: New business owners will need to find their state's requirements for state or franchise tax returns. Many states have different requirements for when these taxes are to be filed and what their rates are. If a state tax is required, a business should know all the dates and other information to ensure the legality of its structure. A listing of each state's requirements for these taxes can be found at the department of taxation office in the state of formation, and most offices have a Web site that lists these requirements as well.

Annual Reports: You will need to find out when your annual reports are due, and this also depends on the state of formation. Some states do not require annual reports, while others have strict schedules as to when businesses are to turn reports in. Some states also have steep late fees if an annual report is past due, adding even more reason for you to know the requirements of your state. A listing of each state's requirements for annual reports can be found on the Secretary of State's Web site. You must register your business for any state business taxes if the state in which your business is formed requires you to do so. If a business has employees, worker's compensation should be filed through the state of the business's formation. Unemployment insurance is another registration that is suggested for a new business, and, although it is not required, it could be a big asset if a new business is unable to survive. Many of these laws and regulations are not readily available to the public, which often leads to businesses being fined or made illegal by their state government. Learning the requirements for individual states only requires a simple online search or a look in the phone book. If you become familiar with all these requirements, you will save money and time and have confidence in the legality of your business.

Resident Agents: After establishing a company's status as a corporation through the incorporation process, you will then need to hire a resident agent. Sometimes these agents are referred to as registered agents or statutory agents. Nearly all states require new businesses to have a resident agent to deal with the legal and tax sides of the structure. In many states, the government will make a business illegal if it does not have a resident agent on staff. Resident agents can be single individuals, lawyers, or service companies designed to provide resident agent services. These individuals take care of all state-based legal issues, allowing individuals to concentrate on running their new business. Resident agents must provide the government with a physical address where they can be contacted any time for legal issues concerning the business they represent. It is their job to keep the business informed as to when they are not in good standing with their state government and tell them the necessary actions to take to be current.

These services are hard to accomplish for business owners because state laws and requirements are constantly changing and can prove difficult to keep up with while running a business. These individuals are also vital commodities if a business is sued because they serve as legal representation and often help to get a better settlement. A resident agent is also suggested for those starting an LLC. The International Association of Commercial Administrators (IACA) is the professional association for those individuals in charge of the overseeing of proper business practices in each state. Most accredited resident agents are members of this organization and use their codes of conduct to govern their work for businesses.

The IACA Web site, at **www.iaca.org**, has a current directory of their members, along with other useful professionals, all listed according to state. The National Conference of Commissioners on Uniform State Laws recently accepted the Model Registered Agents Act to their listing. IACA, along with the American Bar Association, came up with the act, which is also known as the Registered Agents Act, to develop a set standard for resident agents to follow. This law officially states the purpose of resident agents and their functions. The act also defines all terms relating to a resident agent's job.

Federal Requirements: After everything is finished on the state level, you are ready to file the necessary paperwork on the national level. Thankfully, the federal government requires much less paperwork than the state government, and much of the hard work has already been completed and must be transferred over to the national level. The IRS requires businesses to apply for an Employer Identification Number (EIN) to be allowed to operate as legal businesses. All structures, with the exception of sole proprietorships, are required to apply for an EIN, even if the business does not have employees.

There are a number of ways to apply for an EIN, all of which can be found on the IRS's Web site, **www.irs.gov**. The easiest option is to apply online by filling out the Internet EIN application. The application only takes a few minutes, and EINs are issued as soon as the application is validated, minutes after completing the form. The only requirements for this method are for the owners to be legal residents of the United States and have a valid Taxpayer Identification Number, which the IRS names as Social Security number; a different EIN; or an Individual Taxpayer Identification Number.

CHAPTER 7

Expanding Your Business to the Infinite Horizon

Tips from the Experts

Know what days and times to have your listings close. Tuesday is the worst day on eBay and Sunday is the best. The best time is 7-10 p.m. EST. You are not going to do very good if you have stuff closing out at 3 a.m.

— Michael Jordan

Tips from the Experts

I have been incorporated and doing my own designing and artwork since 1981. I have a chronic illness, which means I really need to work at home. I have also found, over the years, that I work very well by myself. I always make sure I get "dressed" for work, even though it may be sweats and a T-shirt. I don't work in pj's. I have found that pj's are not conducive to acting professionally, even if it is just writing eBay listings or answering e-mails.

— Charlene Anderson

First Things First

Before you set up your preferred structure and get all the proper licenses and permits, you need to accomplish certain actions to have a fully operational business. These actions involve the more technical aspects that all businesses face, including what equipment needs to be bought and where the business will be located. These issues are ones that all business owners face, and they must be resolved before any other actions can take place. You can have a beautifully written business plan and have everything else in order, but if you do not have any office equipment or some type of office space, you have nothing.

Accomplishing these two things are the first steps to take toward ensuring a business startup that is smooth and successful. Many people will underestimate how important the smaller details are and will have to pay dearly for it later. This section will help you see the importance of these small steps and explain a way to achieve both, with less stress and in the most cost-efficient way possible.

Although these things seem simple, there are several different choices that must be made for a business to move forward. For example, some business structures will allow for more deductions on rental space and equipment purchases, so it is necessary to become familiar with the particulars of each structure. Business owners need to choose whether they want to work from their home or in an office. If a business owner chooses to set up shop in an office space, he or she will need to decide whether to purchase or lease an office space, along with picking the right location.

Owners will also need to choose between leasing and purchasing office equipment, sort through the deduction possibilities, and choose the option that is right for them. It is also vital that business owners know the proper contracts to fill out for leasing or purchasing, and this section will suggest the important things that need to be included in a contract. This section will also allow you to get a better insight on making these purchases and finding the best option for your business, allowing you to save the most money and take advantage of the most deductions. It will also explain the importance of a "cash flow analysis" and how to go about conducting the proper research to develop a proper analysis that will help you pick the options that will benefit your business the most and will save you the most money.

PowerSelling Tip

In order to stay on top of what is going on in the eBay world, consider visiting www.auctionbytes.com. They have news and blogs about the auction world and eBay. They also offer subscriptions to newsletters with helpful, up-to-date news. Another source is eBay radio, at ***www.wsradio.com/internet-talk-radio.cfm/shows/eBay-Radio.html****.*

Selecting the Right Location for a Business

A business's location can be one of the most important decisions you make; though, the decision is less crucial for eBay business owners, as most of the work is done online. Yet, there are some factors to consider when choosing the location for a business that still pertain to online businesses. There are several options that should be considered before picking a business's location. Although its importance is not as vital as with other businesses, the right location can develop a successful work atmosphere that allows for owners and employees to act in a business-like manner. The right location can also open up possibilities for growth and expansion, and also opening other businesses in the future.

Before choosing a location, it is important for you to first decide whether your business will be located in your home or whether you will work in an office. For an eBay business, either of these options can be successful, but it is imperative that you pick the location that is best for your current situation. You should look at all facets of your business. You should decide how much space you need and whether you want to hire employees. You should also consider whether your home is suitable for a business and whether the presence of the business will cause issues with others living in the house. You should also look at your financial situation and decide whether you can afford to work from an office or will need to do anything to convert your home into a more suitable working environment. It is impossible to list all the planning that should go into making this decision, but if you take the time to sort out all these scenarios, you will be on your way to choosing the right location for your business.

Tips from the Experts

I love working from home and being able to sell my items to the world. I could never get this kind of exposure from a brick-and-mortar store.

— Danna Crawford

Tips from the Experts

I started with a dedicated computer to install the Quicken accounting, Turbo Lister, and shipping software on (I use Endicia for USPS and ShipRush for FedEx) that was near the shipping area. I needed to purchase table weigh scales, storage tubs and racks. Then there are the supplies, like the bubble pack and the water proof bubble pack shipping bags, labels and tape.

— Jim Stewart

Business at Home

You can work from home, but one thing you must check into is local zoning ordinances. These types of ordinances are frequently in neighborhoods to reduce traffic and excessive noise that can arise by having a business next door. A home online business rarely creates excess traffic or noise, so you should not have a problem setting up shop at home. Most of your work will be working online and mailing packages. There will not be many occasions in which a client would come to your home.

It is a good idea to check with your local government office to alleviate any questions or problems in the future. You may need a special permit. It is better to be safe, and then have all your business cards printed with your address on it.

If you do establish your business in your home, it is a good idea to have a separate area set aside for work. This will benefit you in a few ways. For one, it will help you keep organized. It will be hard to keep up with your buyers and the details of their orders if the information is strewn all over your house. Also, it will help you separate work from home. You need time away from work, or it could lead to burnout. Being able to close a door allows you to end your day. In addition, if you have children, they will know that when you are in your "work" area, they should not be a disturbance. If there is no defined area in the home, this can be more difficult to understand.

Finally, if you do choose to operate your business from home, there are a number of deductions that can be taken that cannot be used if the business is in an office. The home-office deduction, which will be discussed in later chapters, allows you to take deductions on office equipment, transportation costs, and even mortgage payments. However, there are some extreme exceptions that will invalidate this deduction, along with strict guidelines to follow, so users must educate themselves before using this deduction. The terms of the home-office deduction can be found on the IRS Web site, at **www.irs.gov**.

Another thing to consider is that government-based research summaries done through the Office of Advocacy found that the IRS treated home-based businesses more harshly than businesses based in offices. To be able to deduct a home office from your taxes, you must use a separate area in your home. We will talk about the IRS and filing later, but for now, make sure you have a defined area in your house. You can only use it for your business to use it as a tax deduction. If you use it for any personal use, you cannot use it as a deduction.

You should consider getting a separate phone for your business. Nothing says unprofessional like when a client calls and gets an answering machine that has a two-year-old stating that you are not home right now. You should have a dedicated answering machine because you will be out in the field often. You may have a cell phone, but this should be used for personal calls, as you do not want clients calling you all times of the day and night.

Tips from the Experts

The reward of being available for my children 24/7 and being able to sell "stuff" to make a living was enough to convince me that it was the perfect career.

— Danna Crawford

Business in an Office

PowerSelling Tip

Remember that the money you make is not yours. It is the business's money. If you spend it like your personal bank account, you will never get ahead and grow your business. Plan on giving yourself a set salary, which can increase as your PowerSeller business grows.

Although working from home has several benefits, there are some people who choose to work outside their home in an office-based setting. People choose this option for various reasons that could include space issues, a large number of employees, or simply a lack of desire to work from home. These individuals must then go about choosing whether they want to buy, rent, or lease a location for their business. If you choose to work outside your home, you will need to decide whether you will purchase or lease your office space. This adds an extra element of work and confusion and must be sincerely thought out before continuing with a new business. It is crucial to weigh all your options and review the benefits and downfalls of each choice before choosing any one method. Most business owners will choose to lease their office space because of its convenience. They will not buy the location because it can be costly and unnecessary. They do this mainly because it will not be able to earn profit for the owner because they are not earning anything from that property.

Leasing is a popular option among business owners, but there are guidelines to follow and steps to take to make the process work correctly. The SBA explains that, since leases are not as highly guarded by consumer protection laws, there is a need to make sure that the terms of a lease are well thought out before signing. The SBA offers a leasing checklist that includes all the necessary procedures needed for a smooth leasing process.

Here is the list of SBA-suggested lease terms, along with a brief explanation of each:

- **Non-compete clause**: The landlord cannot rent out a space near the leased establishment if the other individual is in the same kind of business as the original lessee.

- **Dispute resolution**: Solutions to possible disputes are named in the contract to prevent the landlord and lessee from going to court.

- **Spatial specifications**: Includes the exact measurements of the space being rented.

- **Default and termination**: Conditions for which termination of contract can be allowed.

- **Pets**: Agree whether pets are or are not allowed and whether there will be additional fees due to pets.

- **Rent**: Commercial property rent is always negotiable, so the contract needs to include a price agreed on by both parties, along with reasons for the rent to ever be raised or lowered.

- **Additional costs**: State what utilities, taxes, and upkeep are included.

- **Build outs**: Any improvements that need to be made to the space, including who should pay for which modifications.

- **Sublease**: State whether subleasing will be allowed and whether the landlord will have a say over who subleases the property.

- **Term options**: Add in the option of a short-term lease before signing on for a longer span of time. This is done to see whether the new business is successful before agreeing to pay rent on a space that may no longer be needed. Also include renewal terms and the number of days for the lease to expire.

A clearly written contract is of the utmost importance for business owners to obtain a fair, legal leasing agreement. Once a contract is signed, the rules are set in stone. If you have an issue with any part of your lease contract, you should speak up and start negotiating. Since the landlord and the lessee write these guidelines, having a neutral third party, such as a lawyer, look over the lease contract is recommended. If you carelessly write a lease or sign a lease without thoroughly examining the contents, you may end up stuck in an inadequate, expensive working atmosphere that could cause the business to suffer. Although choosing the right location for a business seems like a minute detail, doing it improperly could severely harm a business. You can prevent this problem by following these requirements and taking extra precautions along the way.

Once you are able to determine the location of your business, and whether you want to lease or buy that property, you then must determine how your office will be run. The most important thing you will need at this point is the proper office equipment to start up and run your business successfully. Although many people do not think that office equipment is important for the success of their business, the following section will squash this misconception and demonstrate the various benefits that the proper office equipment can bring to a growing PowerSeller business.

Tips from the Experts

All I needed were items to sell, a computer, and a camera.

— Danna Crawford

eBay Business Office Equipment

For a business to run successfully, the office space needs to be well stocked with all the necessary equipment and supplies to help the business run more smoothly. Business owners will need to purchase technological equipment, like computers and software, desks and chairs, writing materials, and record books. Many people may already have much of the necessary equipment, especially if their business is based at home, while others may need to purchase all these supplies brand new. No matter the situation, you will need to examine what equipment and supplies are necessary for the successful operation of your business. In this section, we will help shine a light on what is needed for an office space. We will also help distinguish between leasing and buying more expensive equipment by familiarizing you with the basics of leasing and showing the statistics of lessees versus buyers. By the end of this section, you should be able to identify the equipment needs of your business and acquire these resources in the smoothest, most profitable way.

The first thing you should decide on is whether you want to lease or buy your office equipment. Each option has advantages and disadvantages. To make the best decision for your company, you should conduct a cash flow analysis to compare leasing and buying to see which option will allow you to make the most deductions and/or save the most money. This analysis allows you to estimate how much money it would cost to pay off a lease or purchase after taxes. For a cash flow analysis to be successful, you must know the proper terms involved with leasing, purchasing, and financing. You should also be familiar with the rates of your federal and state income taxes.

You should determine how much the equipment is worth and whether it would become an asset to the company. After this, you should determine how long you will lease the product for and the interest rates of buying the equipment. Then, you must determine your cash flow and tax savings for a lease. After these things are found, you can do the proper analysis of your company's assets to find which option will be the most cost-efficient method of acquiring office equipment. Refer back to your business plan to see the sections concerning assets. Once you have determined the value of these assets, they should be recorded in your plan for computation and later reference.

PowerSelling Tip

Two of the most important items that you should have are a measuring stick (or two) and a postage scale.

Leasing

If you choose to lease your office equipment, you can claim depreciation on it. After this depreciation, you can deduct your lease payments on your tax return and end up saving more money than if you had bought the equipment. One of the biggest advantages of leasing office equipment is that leases rarely require you to make a down payment, whereas taking out loans to buy this equipment would require down payments that can get pricey. Leasing is an option for those who are just starting their business and do not have plenty of income coming in. Leasing will allow these individuals to have access to all the office equipment necessary for the success of their business, without paying anything up front. Leasing also allows you to acquire the equipment more easily, as lenders lease out equipment much more quickly than they loan money to pay for it. Also, there are some items that you will not have a long-term need for, and thus, do not need to purchase.

Leased equipment often includes a maintenance plan. This type of plan covers any repairs, and a technician will come out and work on the equipment to keep it running. Look over the contract closely, as there can be hidden fees for these types of services. Some plans even include replacement parts, such as ink cartridges. These items can get pricey, so if you can get them as part of a lease contract at a decent rate, it may well be worth the investment.

Leasing equipment can also give you the advantage of trading up. When your contract is near the time of renewal, many companies will give you updated new equipment. You do not always have this advantage when buying equipment. Equipment can quickly become outdated because of the speed at which technology changes and improves. If you own a piece of equipment, it may quickly lose its value, and you may never get out of it what you invested.

Of course, leasing does have some disadvantages. The cost of leasing equipment will almost always end up costing more than if you had bought the equipment outright. Another downfall of leases is that, once a lease is over, you will have no equity in the equipment because you did not own it. In other words, you will have nothing to show for the money you have spent on the product. In some cases, you will be able to negotiate an agreement in which your lease payments can go toward the purchase price of an item, allowing you to own the equipment over time.

When leasing equipment, there are "inclusion amounts" that come along with leased property. An inclusion amount is an additional cost you must pay each time you deduct your lease on a tax return. If you decide that the benefits of leasing outweigh those of buying, you will need to become familiar with the basic rules of leasing.

Buying

Even with all the advantages that leasing can bring, it could end up costing you more money in the long run. That is why many people choose to buy their office equipment. If you know you will need certain equipment for a long period of time, and you have the means to purchase the equipment, then buying may be your best option.

If you are still having trouble deciding upon your location and equipment, consider the following example, and do the same analysis to your own eBay business. Following is a list of equipment that might be needed for two different eBay businesses. The first is the King PEZ Company. They have a limited budget and are starting their business as a modest, at-home operation. The second is the Queen PEZ Company, and they have a much larger budget, which includes an office and furniture. Both of these are made up, and are used here as examples.

King PEZ

Office Equipment:

Computer, printer $700

Scanner $250

Microsoft Office $350

Intuit QuickBooks $250

PEZ Cataloging Software $30

10 MB Digital Camera/accessories $900

Phone/voice mail/answering machine $200

Postage meter/scale $25

Office Supplies:

Letterhead, envelopes, and business cards $250

Miscellaneous supplies (e.g., pens and folders) $100

Computer/copier paper $50

Read/Write Compact Disks $30

Packing materials $200 (e.g., peanuts, tape, and bubble wrap)

Total $3,350

Queen PEZ

Office Furniture:

Desk, chair, file cabinet(s), and bookcase $3,000

Rent $2,500

Total (including all the other items listed above for King PEZ for just the first month)

$3,350(Office Supplies) + $5,500 (Office Furniture) = $8,850

Let's consider that King PEZ has many items at home already. All they truly need is the postage scale, QuickBooks, and an extra phone, and now their total is $675. There is a huge difference because in an office, you would have to supply everything. The good thing is, you do not need to have a separate office to become a successful eBay business. You must decide, based upon your inventory and volume of business, what the best option is. It is best to lay your two options side by side and decide whether the extra expenses are going to boost your business or are unnecessary start-up and monthly expenses.

Smoking

Smoking is a personal choice; however, as an eBay business, you might want to consider your smoking habits and rules you may want to enforce. Many items will absorb the smell of cigarette or cigar smoke, including the following:

- Clothes
- Cloth
- Books
- Furniture
- Paper products

Any item that is porous and can absorb odors can have the smell of smoke. Many people are opposed to the smell of smoke, or may even be allergic. If your items smell of tobacco smoke or any other strong odor, people can send them back or give you bad feedback. This will hurt your business significantly. You may have items that you bought from elsewhere that smell strongly of smoke or some other odor. There may be little you can do about this, but you may consider posting that information on your listing of the object. This may seem counterproductive, but being honest will increase your credibility.

If you do smoke, you should not smoke around the items you intend to sell, nor should you smoke around packing materials, as cardboard can also absorb the smell of smoke. You can try to seal items in plastic bags. This not only protects your merchandise from odors, but it will also protect them from mice, dust, mold, and moisture.

If you find that your merchandise smells like smoke or some other strong odor, such as perfume, following are some suggestions of how to get rid of the smell. These are only suggestions and should be tried on small samples before using them on large items, as they can ruin certain materials.

If you want to get rid of the smell of smoke in an area of your home or office, try mixing a bucket of water, a half cup of ammonia, a quarter cup of vinegar, and a quarter cup of washing soda, also known as washing ash (This is not to be confused with baking soda). This will make a cleaning solution. Start from the bottom and work your way up the walls, counters, and even the ceiling, if you are able. You will need to wash you curtains with ammonia in the washing machine, as this will neutralize the smell. If you have lamp shades or other hanging items, you may want to consider replacing them.

Consider that your carpet absorbs almost everything in the environment. If you cannot afford to replace the carpet, and the carpet pad underneath, you can steam clean or shampoo your carpets. Make sure that you vacuum on a regular basis with a decent vacuum cleaner that has a HEPA filter. You can also try sprinkling baking soda on a carpet and allowing it to set for a day or two. This will allow the soda to absorb the smoke odor, and then you can vacuum it. When washing fabrics, you can add some baking soda or use detergents that already contain baking soda.

Vinegar is a natural, effective way to cut through the dirt and tar that smoke can leave behind. It not only destroys the smell, but can help items look less dingy. Be careful using vinegar on fabric, as it can destroy it. Try it on a sample piece or on a part of the fabric that will not show.

Some cleaning and deodorizing agents only mask the odor with other strong smelling odors rather than cleaning or getting rid of the smoke residue. Febreze is a product that does work. It contains a chemical compound called cyclodextrin that absorbs odors, similar to baking soda. Again, make sure that what you are spraying it on will not be damaged. You should also look for products that contain activated charcoal. Charcoal also works as a chemical that will absorb smoke and other strong smells on objects.

One the best things you can do to rid a closed space of a smoke smell is to open up the windows and doors. A breeze will loosen odor particles and take them away. You can do this whenever you have a product that you have purchased for resale that smells like smoke.

Ozone-based electronic air cleaners can work wonders, as they remove smoke and other odor-causing particles from the air. They can range in price, but even a small, inexpensive unit can work wonders.

The Internet provides multiple ways to expand your business to the farthest frontiers. If you want to be a major player in the online business world, you are eventually going to have to start thinking about reaching out and casting a wider net. If you put a little bit of time and energy into planning how you are going to accomplish all these agendas, you will be surprised at the returns. Some of these things you will be able to do yourself, but for other things, you are most likely going to need to hire some professionals.

The following tips and strategies are not for the beginner. Nothing is more hurtful to your business than spending time expanding your customer base, only for those customers to find that you do not have what they are looking for. Although, you do not need to be an eBay PowerSeller to take advantage of all these powerful tools, you should make sure that you have a strong product line and the mechanisms to serve your customer efficiently and effectively. Spend plenty of time building up your business and your product lines before expanding with the following steps.

Keyword Marketing

The easiest of these strategies to put into practice is likely keyword marketing. Imagine that you are looking for something that you sell, and pretend to be an eBay buyer. Most people become sellers by being buyers anyway, but the goal of this is to see whether you can easily find your product amid a sea of other vendors offering similar products.

Take note of which vendors seem to come up first, and who has chosen the best use of keywords for their products. Use this time to modify how you market your products with your keywords. It is not always as easy as people may think it is to find something that you want on eBay. Chances are, somewhere someone has what you are looking for, but unless you choose the right keywords for your search, you may never know that it is there. Choose your keywords carefully.

Take time choosing your text carefully. Use as many keywords as possible in both the title of you product and the text of the entire posting. Resist the temptation to keyword SPAM by using either irrelevant or fraudulent keywords. Nothing will upset a customer more than when they are looking for the latest PlayStation® game when your antique china lamps come up because of the misuse of keywords. Use as many keywords as you can, but make sure they are relevant.

Titles

Choose your titles carefully; your text will be how potential buyers find you using either Google or eBay search engines. Because of this, your titles should be loaded with keywords. Nonetheless, avoid those common, annoying clichés that cause many products to get lost. Avoid the repeating line of exclamation points, and the "Wow" or other such trite catchphrases. Be fresh, be unique, and use as many relevant keywords as possible.

Watch your Tone

Make sure your words are always professional in tone and grammatically correct. You do not want to sound like you are their friend or a street vendor; you are a professional salesperson, and you should sound like one. If you need help with your grammar, check out Grammar Girl's Quick and Dirty Tips for Better Writing at **http://grammar.quickanddirtytips.com/** and Purdue University's online writing lab (OWL) at **http:// owl.english.purdue.edu/**. Both resources will significantly increase the quality of your writing.

You do not need to sound snobbish or stuffy, so feel free to use a light, conversational tone; just use proper English. The only exception to this rule would be selling to teenagers, or if you have an especially specific target audience who primarily speaks in a particular slang or dialect. Though, caution must be exercised; it is always better to err on the side of caution and not overdo it on the slang. A little bit here and there is okay, but you will find that even people who normally speak in a slang will be more likely to respect and trust someone who speaks properly than another person who is trying to speak "their language."

The Power of Words

Your business is built on words. Words are the lifeblood of your eBay store, so make sure you use them correctly. The more professional a seller is, the more detailed they are with their eBay text and product descriptions. Also, fill the body of your product descriptions with keywords. It does not make for the most interesting descriptions, but you can still make it fresh, detailed, and professional. And better yet, if you have a high keyword density, your product will be more likely to come up as one of the first when customers do a search.

Selling from Your Web Site

Outside of eBay, there are several strategies that can help drive up sales. After you have somewhat established yourself on eBay, it may be time to become an expert. Publishing an informational Web site that offers tons of free advice and enjoyable articles, and fosters discussion, can be an excellent way to increase your total sales. It may take some time and effort on your part, but in the end, it will pay off if you do everything correctly. You will be amazed at the power information has to generate sales.

For instance, say Mario is the owner of an eBay fine wine and liquor store called WinesSoFine. He decides that he is going to publish an informational Web site about fine wine and dining. His first step is to go do some research; he may have some amount of knowledge already, but now he wants to become an expert. He goes to the bookstore, he goes to the library, he does some Internet research, and he makes lists of all the knowledge he has gained. He does not plagiarize any of this, but rather, he uses all this information and puts it into his own voice and words. His computer is a Mac, and it comes with a free Web site hosting package called iWeb, so soon, he is up and running. He has about ten pages of information, all dealing with various aspects of wine connoisseurship. On every page, he has links to his eBay store, and he has gotten into the habit of giving out free information and tips to people who come to his site and use his prominently displayed e-mail address and contact information. Soon, Mario is seeing more customers buying his products online than ever before.

This increase in sales is happening because Mario has established himself as an expert in the field. People have come to trust him and enjoy reading his online articles. People do not like to buy things from people whom they do not trust and know. For instance, Radio Shack is a known vendor of electronics. People will be much more likely to buy from them than from Billy Bob's Discount Electronics Warehouse, even if they sell almost exactly the same merchandise and Billy Bob offers better prices. Radio Shack has been around for years, and they hire motivated, knowledgeable people who have proven to be well-versed in the products they sell.

Mario has just done the same. He has given himself staying power in the online world, and also increased his total sales, all by creating a ten-page Web site that he only has to maintain with small updates. By creating one or several online informational sites geared toward products you sell, you can do your business an incredible benefit.

Creating Your Informational Web Site

Step 1: Choose Your Product Category

Take some time considering what category of products your Web site will focus on. Ask yourself questions, like what your angle and spin is going to be. What are you going to name your site? Are there books written about your subject? What about other Web sites touching on similar topics? Take some time to learn as much as you can about what your Web site is going to contain.

For instance, say you deal in vintage comic books. You can develop a wonderfully informative Web site about your own love for collecting comics, how to collect them, some things every collector should know, what some of the rarest comics out there are, and a host of other juicy tidbits that would be entertaining and informative to your niche audience.

The wonderful thing about hiring writers is that you can hire them to write articles for your site following the keyword format. You can give them the keywords that you want them to use, and also links to some of your research, or you can give them a link to an Internet keyword selector tool, which counts how many times a word was searched. Professional writers can make the keyword articles sound interesting, and they can seamlessly integrate the keywords into the articles so that Google's censors will not flag and possibly delete your site. It pays to hire a professional, especially when dealing with keywords.

Step 2: Build and Publish

After you have all the content written, you are going to want to build and publish your Web site. There are many good Web site developing programs out there, and many computers come with one already installed. For instance, if you own a Mac, they have excellent web developing software called iWeb, which makes building a professional-looking Web site a breeze.

Stay away from services that are going to cost you much, as there are many quality programs that are essentially free. The ones that do not cost you anything, like freewebs.com, make money by selling advertising space on your site. If you do not mind ads, their sites are professional and easy to develop. Though, there are other programs you can use that are also exceedingly good and do not involve ads, but they will cost you a little money, like the program SiteSpinner.

Always use keywords in the name of your site and in the header.

Step 3: Onward to the Search Engines

Now that you have done the hard work of becoming an expert on your product, you have plenty of content, and your Web site looks awesome, the only thing left is to make sure people will actually get to see it. The way you do that is by submitting your Web site to all the major search engines, which is not as hard as it may sound. All the search engines have specific instructions on how you should submit your site to their index. The three major search engines that your site must be on are Google, Yahoo, and MSN. The others do not measure up to these big three, and if you can get your site to come up on these, then you are almost certain to come up on the smaller ones as well.

Be wary of services that offer to submit your Web site for you for a fee. You can do it yourself, and it will not cost you anything. If you do not have the time, just stay away from the services promising to post you on hundreds of search engines. It would be terrific if more people used some of the lesser-known search engines, but they do not, so stick with a legitimate service that understands the value of getting you on the top three.

About Me

Do not underestimate the power of your "About Me" page. Especially if you ever want to become a big PowerSeller, you must use this free feature from eBay for all that it is worth. Buying things online is always somewhat of a risky endeavor. You have no idea whether the person on the other side of the Internet is a legitimate business owner or is trying to scam you.

Your About Me page is your chance to introduce yourself to the world. As an online business owner, you must be willing to sacrifice some of your privacy. Use this page to talk about yourself. Why did you get into this business in the first place? If you sell craft supplies, when did your "love affair" with home craft projects first begin? What are some of your hobbies? If you know how to do it, include some pictures of yourself looking like a happy person that the online customer would love to get to know.

Make sure you include your contact information: a phone number, your physical location, your e-mail, and your name. Experts agree that no one should buy things from a seller who will not provide this basic information. You might want to consider getting a P.O. Box if you are uneasy giving out your home address; if you have a storefront, just use that address. If you do not already have a business e-mail, go ahead and get one. Yahoo, Google, and MSN are again the easiest e-mail options.

Tips from the Experts

"My eBay" is the home base for my business record keeping. eBay has made life much easier for sellers with the customized tools for setting up our "My eBay" center. I stress to my students how this can be set up to meet all your needs as a seller. In addition to the reports available, eBay has made record keeping a breeze compared to the old pen and paper days of keeping track.

— Danna Crawford

Other eBay Selling Venues

As you expand your business, there may be some other venues to consider other than just **eBay.com**. eBay has expanded their company and now has affiliate companies with which you can sell items. Part of the reason is that certain products, like car sales, became so large that they required a site dedicated to just those products. Here is a list of other affiliate sites and a brief explanation of each.

eBay Motors

This site is dedicated to selling just cars. The format is almost identical to eBay.com. Make sure you read all the policies and rules before you begin selling, because there are some differences. You can access the site at www.motors.eBay.com. Many of the cars listed are by people who are private parties. Dealers also sell on here, but usually place special or hard-to-find cars with special accessories. The bidding and selling structure is pretty much the same as it is on eBay.com.

Half.com

This site is dedicated to selling print and multimedia items, such as books, DVDs, video games, and CDs. There is no bidding involved, and there are no bidding fees either. This is quite advantageous if your products fall into these categories. You can sell your items for any amount you like, but Half.com does give you a suggested selling price once you put the information about the book in the listing. You can do this by using the UPC or ISBN code on the product. Here is what Half.com suggests selling your products for, according to their condition. The percentages are based on the retail price of the item.

- Like New 50%
- Very Good 45%

- Good 40%
- Acceptable 35%

You should be aware that your item must have a UPC code or ISBN number that is recognized by Half.com's catalog. If you cannot locate the number, or they do not have it in their catalog, you should consider selling the item on eBay.com instead.

There are no listing fees. However, should you sell an item on Half.com, they do take a commission. Here is a breakdown of their commission structure:

- $0.75 - $50.00 = 15.0%
- $50.01 - $100.00 = 12.5%
- $100.01 - $250.00 = 10.0%
- $250.01 - $500.00 = 7.5%
- > $500.00 = 5.0%

These rates are determined per item sold and do not include the price of shipping. Payments to sellers are sent twice a month to the place designated, such as a direct deposit to a checking account. Shipping is handled a bit differently than it is on eBay.com. Half.com charges a flat rate and reimburses the seller this amount in their twice-a-month payments. They have two options for the buyer — Media Mail and Expedited. They can get a slight discount if they buy more than one item at once. Be aware that what Half.com charges the buyer for shipping and what they reimburse the buyer are two different amounts. To find information regarding shipping rates, go to **http://pages.half.eBay.com/help/policy/shipping_p.html**.

StubHub

This site allows people to buy and sell event tickets. You can buy and sell tickets on eBay.com, but StubHub works a little differently. First, there is no auctioning involved with StubHub. You set the price for what you want to charge for the tickets. This can have advantages and disadvantages. You will get what you want for your event tickets, but you may have fewer interested buyers.

The way it works is that if a person wants to buy your tickets, they will pay for them on the StubHub site. You will have 48 hours to confirm the sale. If you do not respond, or you no longer have the tickets, StubHub will help the buyer find alternative tickets. If you do have the tickets and confirm, you then have to send the tickets immediately. You will be paid seven days later by check or PayPal after StubHub confirms that the client received the tickets. StubHub guarantees that the buyer will receive their tickets in time for the concert, and you have to ship accordingly. The good news is that the buyer pays the shipping, and StubHub will send you the FedEx sticker to mail the ticket.

Before you set up business as a ticket broker for StubHub, be aware that there are laws concerning the resale of tickets in certain states. You can check **www.stubhub.com/help-top-questions-seller** to see what the current state laws are. Some states only allow you to sell the ticket for $3 over the face value of the ticket, so unless you were getting the tickets for a fantastic deal to start, you will not make much of a profit.

Kijiji

This site is owned by eBay and is a classified advertising site. You can list advertise your products on this site for free, much like the classified ads section of a newspaper or like **www.craigslist.com** . This site has some designs that are similar to eBay when viewing products, accept this site is not set up for bidding. You can search by city and state when you first log on. Then you can search under various categories like housing, personal ads, or for sale items. You can also search for items by keyword. This site is worth checking out, **www.kijiji.com**. You can sell your items to different regions, and it is especially helpful if you have a retail store. It is not moderated like eBay is, and the buyers contact you directly. If you are having a hard time selling particular items on eBay, this maybe your solution. If you sell locally you also eliminate shipping costs.

MicroPlace

This eBay-owned company has jumped on the bandwagon of microloans. If you have some extra cash, and you want to make some money while helping people out, you should check out this site, at **www.microplace.com**.

Here is the way micro lending works. People are in need worldwide and are in poverty situations. They would not qualify for a regular loan to help them work or start a business. Micro lending takes the investments of many people and organizations and then lends out this money to people in these dire situations. You make your money back as they pay back their loan. There is some risk involved as with any loan situation. You should look at the fine print before loaning any money. The good part is that you are not loaning large amounts of money to a couple of people, rather you are loaning small amounts to many different people.

Placing the information that you invest part of your profit into the working poor on your site helps boost the class of your business. It makes people think that the money they are spending on products sold by you is going to a good cause. The best part about it is that you are making a small profit by helping others in need.

ProStores

This eBay-owned site is for those ready to set up a Web store. They offer competitive prices, compared to other online web site servers. They have a variety of different levels of Web sites and services available depending on the needs and size of your company. The nice part about using this site to set up your store is that it is eBay friendly and they offer you a unique web address. Once you set up the site, ProStores automatically imports your live eBay listings and other settings. You can access this site at **www.prostores.com/ecommerce_eBay.html**.

Skype

Nothing says classy and cutting edge like the ability for your customers to be able to chat with you online. Skype is a free service that allows you to make regular and video calls around the world. If the call is from one Skype user to another, the call is free. You can also call cell phones and landlines for next to nothing. Skype offers an incoming number and voicemail for just dollars a month.

Your buyers can look for the Skype logo on your listing. They can click the "chat" button, which is in a text format, or the "voice" button. It will let them know when you are online to answer questions. As a PowerSeller, you can indicate whether you want to be contacted with chat or voice on the "Sell Your Item" process.

Having this option available makes your buyers more confident that you can be contacted and that you are a real person selling an item. You can connect with previous buyers easily and make them repeat customers more easily. You do not even have to be online to receive a Skype call, as there is a forwarding function that allows you to receive your call almost anywhere.

Setting up Skype on eBay is not that difficult. First you will need to make sure you have the latest version of Skype. You can find the free software at **www.skype.com**. You must create an account on Skype; this is free unless you add other services. You can link your Skype account to your eBay account by going to your eBay account and looking for Skype in your eBay preferences.

Under your preferences in the "My eBay" tab, select "Member-to-Member Communications." It is here that you can "Add" a Skype Name to update your preferences. On your Skype account, click "link my Skype account to eBay".

Once you have added Skype to your preferences, Open Skype, and click Tools > Options > Privacy. You need to make sure that you select the "Allow my status to be shown on the Web" check box. As you create a new listing, you should add your Skype name, and buyers can contact you quickly via Skype.

Looking Out for What is Hot

PowerSelling Tip

If you want to know what the hottest items to sell are, look at magazines, newspapers, and television to determine trends. Keep a pad handy to jot down ideas as you see them. Teenagers can also be an untapped resource. Teens usually know what is hot and what is not. They are your greatest resource for trends and items that everyone is trying to get their hands on.

One of the greatest pages that can help keep you on top is **http://pulse.eBay.com**. eBay pulse has two main columns. The first is the most popular searches on eBay. This has key words that people are searching for, and it gives you a countdown of the top ten.

The second column is the top five companies currently on eBay. This is based upon sales. You should strive to get your business on this list, or at least you can see which companies are doing well. You can click on them and study their site, their company, and their auctions to see what ideas you can generate to improve your business.

You can look at specific categories of items to see what their top companies and searches are. At the bottom of the Web page are the most watched items.

This page can help you determine trends and ways to increase sales, such as using keywords for your listings.

Seller Central

The Seller Central page has loads of useful information and links for you to view and use. It is designed to help you accelerate your PowerSeller business. It lists some of the more helpful links that can help you upgrade your business to the next level.

eBay Idea House

This is a tool for first time sellers, but even for a PowerSeller, it is worth looking at. It takes you to different rooms in your house and gives you ideas about items there that you might consider selling. For a PowerSeller, this can give you new avenues to consider for listings.

CHAPTER 8

Open Doors by Raising Your "Status" Quo

There are a number of things you can do in order to look more like a legitimate business. This is important because buyers will usually buy from businesses that do not look like they are in someone's garage somewhere.

Buyer Security

Consumer awareness of fraud is at an all-time high, and there is some natural reluctance to make a purchase from an unknown seller. You can ease that fear with tools like online escrow or bonding guarantees.

PayPal Protection

Being able to display the "PayPal Protection" icon on your Web page will also enhance your credibility considerably. Showing this icon and being part of that program will offer your buyers a little more reassurance that you are legit, and they are going to get what they expect.

PayPal Protection is a program that offers up to $1,000 in protection for items that are not received. You have to have a PayPal business or premier account to offer this protection, and you also have to have at least 50 feedback comments and a 98 percent positive rating. The best thing about this program is that it is free.

Escrow Services

If you are selling high-dollar items, buyers have even more reason to be cautious and mistrusting. Usually, when you are selling ordinary, low-value items for $5 or $10, you receive payment first, and then ship out the item. But suppose you are selling something for $1,000. The buyer does not want to send you the money without getting the item in hand first, but you, as the seller, do not want to send out the item without receiving payment first. Escrow services provide a handy way to overcome this mutual distrust.

Both parties deal through the escrow agent. You send the item to the escrow agent, not the customer. The customer sends payment to the escrow agent, not you. The escrow agent, once satisfied that both parties have met their obligations, will then make the transfer. The buyer will have an agreed-upon amount of time to inspect the item before payment is transferred from the escrow agent to the seller.

Of course, even an escrow service can be crooked, so you need to find one that is reputable and has an established name, such as **www.Escrow.com**, which is approved by eBay. Naturally, there is an extra fee involved, which may be up to 3 percent of the sale price. It is up to you and the buyer to decide who pays the escrow fee. You may decide to cover the cost or agree to split the cost, although some sellers insist that the buyer bear the entire cost.

There have been some fraudulent operators who have pretended to be escrow services. Proceed with caution. If you have never heard of the escrow service, do some investigating before using their services, or just stick with the ones that have an established reputation.

Bonding Guarantees

This is another type of guarantee that offers reassurance to sellers, and also is useful for those who are dealing in high-value items. Like escrow services, it is not really worth the extra expense if you are dealing in $10 or $20 goods.

Bonding is a type of insurance policy. It provides a guarantee to the buyer that if the seller does not fulfill his or her obligation, the bonding agency will satisfy that obligation one way or another, usually with a refund. One such reputable bonding guarantee service is BuySAFE, at **www.buysafe.com**, which is often used for eBay transactions.

BuySAFE has a new program for eBay Trading Assistants. They offer the following advantages on their Web site:

- Beat the competition and increase revenue
- Attract more valuable consignment merchandise
- Appear first in TA search, as a featured Trading Assistant
- Meet eBay's Registered eBay Drop Off Location (REDOL) insurance requirement for carrying a $25,000 bond

They are offering this service due to problems with dropping off merchandise with a Trading Assistant (TA) or REDOL. eBay now requires that REDOLS become licensed and/or bonded.

To offer bonding guarantees, you apply with the bonding agency, and they evaluate your application and do various background checks on you. You pay a fee and then display the logo from the bonding agent on your Web site. The BuySAFE logo is common, and many buyers will recognize it, giving them a greater level of confidence in your online store.

Buyers do not have to pay a fee to enjoy the protection of the bonding agent. You, as seller, pay a fee that is equal to a percentage of the transaction — usually about 1 percent. The fee applies only when goods are actually sold; if an auction item goes unsold, then you do not have to pay. You can also decide to apply the protection to all your auctions or only to select auctions. Many sellers decide to use the bonding guarantee only for higher-value auctions.

Square Trade

Another common logo is the "SquareTrade" logo, which is another tool that helps to create confidence. Square Trade is not part of eBay, but is recommended by eBay. It is simply a dispute resolution agency that helps in case a seller and buyer have a disagreement. There is a $20 fee for resolution services. Even if the fee wipes out your profits, it may still be worthwhile to pay it because if the dispute is resolved amicably, you may be able to have negative feedback removed. That is worth much more than $20. Too much negative feedback can kill an eBay business quickly.

You may be able to qualify to display the SquareTrade "seal of approval." Displaying the logo on your auction pages will create confidence. Of course, if you are a holder of the SquareTrade seal, SquareTrade checks your feedback and reports periodically to make sure you continue to be a legitimate seller. They will take back their seal if they suspect foul play. Buyers know this, of course, so displaying the seal is of great value.

Certified Provider Program

eBay offers a program that helps set a group of providers aside that help eBay users grow their businesses through services, including technology or data licensing services. In order to be certified, you must meet criteria at both the company level and the individual staff level in specific areas of expertise. eBay offers an educational program that leads to better understanding of eBay, its applications, practices, and policies. This not only increases your credibility, it gives you an edge over the competition, as you will understand eBay from an internal level.

You must also show eBay a certain level of experience and expertise in order to become certified. There are two different levels of certification. With each level, you will be able to display a special logo on your site, business, and listings.

PowerSelling Tip

An example of certified software is DeepAnalysis, which helps you look at auctions and tells you which items sell the most and which deliver the best income. You can do a Google search to find out which sites you can download this software from.

Service Provider Level

This level shows that you perform tasks like responding to buyer inquiries, you design your store and listing templates in a way that solidifies your brands, and you are able to provide suggestions about the best ways to sell products on eBay. In order to achieve this level of certification, you must:

- Pass individual exams
- Have customer references
- Have a verified commitment to excellence on eBay

Solution Provider Level

In this level, you should be able to provide technology and eBay data related solutions. You should be able to perform tasks based on the technology you create or data you license. Some of the areas this includes are building software applications and licensing data to support customer needs.

In order to achieve this level of certification you must do the following:

- Pass individual Exams
- Have customer references
- Have a verified commitment to excellence on eBay
- Have either a standard application or a certified application, and if you use eBay data, a Market Data License

Here are some of the benefits to becoming a Certified Service Provider or Solution Provider.

- Using their logo.
- An upgraded search display and an upgraded detail display.
- An advertising credit.
- Being included in the Solutions Directory, at **http://cgi6.eBay.com/ws/eBayISAPI.dll?SolutionsDirectory**.
- Being included on the Certified Provider site, at **http://certified-provider.eBay.com**.
- Site Marketing. Each solution type on the Certified Provider site is promoted in rotating ads on Seller Hub, Seller Central, and in "My eBay" to each solution type.
- eBay staff training and awareness. This benefit gives you influence internally in the company. You will be able to present to key stakeholders at eBay what sets you apart from other providers. You will be able to influence them first hand as to why they should recommend your solutions directly to their high-volume accounts.

- Education Specialist training and awareness. eBay has hundreds of instructors in the Education Specialist training and influences many users of eBay every year.

- The ability to conduct Certified Provider led workshops.

- Business and Technical training. This training educates and informs employees and contractors about eBay features, policies, best practices, and technology.

- Being eligible for Consultant certification and Engineer certification. This certification allows you to certify your staff, which has the potential to increase sales for your company.

This certification does not come cheap. Currently, the yearly fee for being a Certified Provider is $3000/Year. For Consultant or engineer certification, it costs $150/Individual. For a certification retest, it is $75/Individual. If you are interested in the certification program, you can go to **http://developer.eBay.com/programs/certifiedprovider/apply** for an application and information.

PowerSelling Tip

Do you want to know what is hot and what is not in the world to help you with some ideas of what to sell? Check out ***http://buzz.yahoo.com/****. This site lists all the top stories, items, and words that have received the most searches that day. Another site to check is* ***http://www.google.com/trends****. It is similar in that it lists hot trends that day in the world.*

CHAPTER 9

Streamlining Your Finances

A strong financial mind will not only keep you afloat, it is the key to creating a business that will grow by leaps and bounds. This chapter is about cutting corners where you can and keeping your expenses lean.

There are endless expenses and fees as an eBay seller. If you do not keep track of these little nuisances, your business could be in danger. Many of these expenses are minor. When you are running a small business, you have a tendency to overlook minor expenses, but in the end, they add up and can easily eat up all your profits before long.

Big Money Consumers

In business, we speak of profit centers and cost centers. These terms are self-explanatory. Certain functions are done to generate profit directly. Others support the overall business, indirectly generating profit, and their main purpose is spending the company's money.

Cost centers can be found in unusual places and can become a problem. It is essential to keep track of them and minimize those costs whenever possible. In an eBay business, the three biggest common cost centers are:

- eBay listing fees
- Packing and shipping material

- Staff (for larger eBay businesses)
- Storage/office space

I will not include the actual cost of the goods you are selling here. That would fall more in the category of "cost of goods sold," and is more of a direct, profit-generating expense rather than a mere cost center. There are, of course, countless other minor cost centers, including office supplies, software, and legal/accounting services, and each must be regulated closely.

Hiring an accounting service is a nice convenience, but if your business is still small, you could easily spend your entire profit on an accountant. Do the books yourself until your business has grown large enough to merit outsourcing the function.

There is, of course, a fundamental difference between a small business and a large one, and that is the concept of "do it yourself." As a small business owner, you will need to start out doing your own accounting, filing some of your own legal/organizational papers, running your own errands, and serving as everything from floor sweeper to CEO. There is a natural temptation to want to outsource these jobs immediately, but you must resist. Outsourcing these functions too early in your small business will result in a much longer period before you are profitable. If you are like most small businesspersons, you do not have bags of money on hand to subsidize a failing business for long.

eBay Listing Fees

One of the loudest complaints of PowerSellers is the eBay listing fees. There are many different things you can spend money on with eBay, and the listing fees can rapidly consume a large share of your profits, if you are not careful.

The easiest way to fail on eBay is to list absolutely everything you have without paying attention to whether you think it will sell. It is easy to think, "Well, if it doesn't sell, I've only lost the listing fee." But when you multiply that $1 or $2 times hundreds of items, you have spent a significant amount of money to list things that are not selling.

Suppose your average listing fee is $1 per item. That does not sound like much to risk, but in reality, it is more than $1 if you are not selling every single thing you list, and most people do not. If you list 100 items and sell 5 of them, you have not really spent $1 per item. You have spent $20 per item. Consider also that the listing fee of a $1 item is 35 cents. If you list it at 99 cents instead, the listing fee is 15 cents. The fee jumps up to 55 cents after $9.99, so if you are selling items under $10, list them a little lower to save yourself money. The greatest jump in listing fees occurs when you get to $25 and the listing fee is $1. At $24.99, the fee is $0.35. If you then go to $50, it is $2 for the listing fee, but this does not change until you get to $200, when the fee is $3. The best, most economical ranges for selling to keep your fees reasonable are under $24.99 and above $49.99. To see what the current fee structure is you can go to **http://pages.eBay.com/help/sell/fees.html**.

The most important ratio here is not the amount of listing fees per item listed, but the amount of listing fees divided by the items that have been sold. You do not need to do the full treatment for every single item. There are extra cents to be paid for every bold listing, every extra photo, and every special placement. Use those extra eBay features sparingly. If you have a high-dollar item likely to attract attention, spend the extra money to get the prominent listings, but it is wasteful to take that approach with every single item you have.

There are many options you can take advantage of on your eBay listings, but unfortunately, almost all of them cost extra. The basic auction listing is reasonably priced, but limited. On the other hand, if you add too many of the extra options, your listing fees can eat up your profits.

If you are selling Books, Music, DVDs and Movies, or Video Games, there is a fixed insertion price of 15 cents, and 35 cents for other types of items.

This is also important to know for final fees explained below. Fixed-priced items are similar to Buy It Now Auctions.

PowerSelling Tip

You can set a reserve price for a listing, which can protect you from selling your item too cheaply. This allows you to set the bidding price low. The reserve has to be met in order for the item to be sold on the auction. The buyers do not see the reserve price; they only see the current bid. When buyers see a low auction price, they will be more likely to bid. Be careful not to set your reserve price too high or no one will win the listing. If you do decide to use a reserve price, you will be charged $2 extra for items up to $199.99 and 1 percent of the reserve price for items $200 and over.

Buy It Now

This is a good option if you want to offer a product at a set price. Many eBay stores use this to sell items at a set price that they sell frequently. This service also attracts those buyers that want to buy an item right now and do not want to wait for an auction to be completed. To use the Buy It Now listing, it will cost no more than 25 cents, depending on the selling price of the item. The other advantage for the seller is that the customer has to pay for the item immediately when purchasing this way. Like any other item you sell, make sure that you do not set your price too high. As a rule of thumb, you can always start the listing price of an auction item for the amount you bought it for. This protects your investment. For setting your Buy It Now price, look at other listings of the same or similar item and see what your competition is selling their items for.

Final Fees

There two different types of final fees. There are the auction-style fees and the fixed fees.

The auction-style fees are for most auctions and are at least 8.75%. The price goes down slightly after $25 to $1,000. You must consider these fees, as you will have to pay them on each item you sell, and therefore, you must try to calculate them into your price.

For fixed-priced items, the amount varies between 6 and 15 percent, depending on the item, so pay close attention to the list on **http://pages.eBay.com/help/sell/fees.html**.

Upgrades

There are different upgrades that can be added to your listing. In the chapter dealing with adding photos, I mention that after the first picture, eBay begins charging. It is nice to have a number of pictures of your item, but you must think about what it is costing you.

There is a free option for the Gallery. This places a small picture of your item with your listing. It is placed next to the item title and is a nice way to attract your buyers. You should use this option with every listing. You can make the image larger using Gallery Plus for an extra 35 cents.

You can add bold type to your listing. This will cost you $2 per listing. It will boldface your listing, but may not always be worth the extra cost. A similar feature is a subtitle that can provide descriptive information on your item below the main title that buyers will see when browsing categories or viewing search results. This service costs 50 cents a service. You can highlight your item for $5 or add a border for $4 a listing. These kinds of add-ons are for items in which many sellers are selling the same item, and you want to stand out.

If you want help jazzing up your listing, you can use the Listing Designer feature for an additional 10 cents. You can add a background theme and attractive design to your listing.

If you want listings to appear during a special promotion or event, you can use the "Schedule Your Listing" feature which allows you to list items up to three weeks in advance. The cost of this service is 10 cents per listing. There is a gift upgrade that will list your item under eBay's gift listings for an additional 25 cents.

If you really want to make sure that your buyers see your item first, you can pay an extra $24.95 for the chance that your item will be listed on the first page of a buyer's search results of an item. If you want your item to be featured on eBay's homepage, it will cost you $59.95.

The prices of these services are subject to change, so you should look at **http://pages.eBay.com/help/sell/fees.html** to see what the current offerings are.

Packing and Shipping Material

The price for packing material and boxes varies considerably. If you buy your boxes and packing material at the local drugstore, you are likely to be paying at least ten times what you should be paying for it. You can easily go down to your local drugstore or supermarket and spend $4 or $5 just to buy a single box and enough bubble wrap and filler material to send a single package. Many people are not even making $5 on average for each item they sell. Sure, local department stores and drugstores have these items, and it is convenient for people who have only one or two things to ship, but you are running a business. You need to buy these items in large quantities from large office supply stores or specialty suppliers.

Many eBay sellers do not even keep track of shipping material costs, but you must. Some of the biggest dot-com failures of the recent boom collapsed precisely for this reason — their fulfillment costs exceeded their profits. Shipping materials will be one of your largest expenses, so it is worthwhile to devote some time to comparing prices for boxes, bubble wrap, and filler material at your local office supply stores, where you will find the best deals locally. There are also some eBay sellers who specialize in selling these sorts of materials to other eBay sellers, so check on eBay directly as well. With little effort, it will be possible to cut your fulfillment costs. Remember that the USPS offers free boxes if you want to ship priority, and you can even order boxes with the eBay logo.

Tips from the Experts

Right now, I run my $450,000 eBay/Internet business with two employees and a few outsourced helpers that do occasional work for me. I have a small office that can hold about three or four of us at a time and our entire eBay inventory. It's working out well.

— Jim Cockrum

Staff

If your growth ambitions are realized, you will need to hire some staff at some point. As with any expenditure, avoid hiring staff prematurely, as this can be a major expense. As with many businesses, eBay may be cyclical. There will be downtimes and uptimes. There will be times of the year when you have more business than you can handle, but there will also be times when it is slow. This is the natural cycle of any sort of business, especially in direct sales. However, employees tend to expect regular hours, which creates a dilemma. Ideally, you would like to have an employee who would come in whenever you need them and leave when the work is done; there is nothing more frustrating to an employer than seeing an employee with nothing to do. But for most employees, the ideal is the exact opposite — regular hours, same time every week, same number of hours. I hope you can find a happy medium that satisfies both parties.

Following are some types of employees you might want to consider as your eBay business grows:

- If you have an office with a few employees, you might consider an office manager. They can take care of day-to-day administrative, clerical, and office supply duties.

- As you grow, you may need another seller to take care of the auctions online. This person should have experience selling on eBay and be dedicated to your business. Be sure to check a number of references closely before hiring this person, as they could help or destroy your businesses name and reputation.

- If you need someone to do packing, you might consider hiring a part-time or full-time packer. This person should be good at packing and have good spatial skills. You want them to be able to pack to minimize your costs and ensure that the package arrives intact.

- If you are running a large, high-profile company, you may need to hire a public relations (PR) person to take care of talking to clients, distributors, or the general public. They must be diplomatic, have good communication skills, and be able to answer questions under pressure.

- If you do not have time to market your company, you can hire a freelance, part-time, or full-time marketing manager. They can take care of advertising, promotion, analyzing the market, and steering your company in the right direction.

- If you just want to hand over the financial aspects of your business to someone who has a love for numbers, then you may consider hiring a bookkeeper. This should be someone with some education and experience. Sometimes, a retired bookkeeper who is looking for some part-time work may be your best option.

- If you like making a mess, but not cleaning it up, you may consider hiring a cleaning service. This person helps clean your area and the storage area. This can ensure items are clean and that there are no pests to worry about.

- You might need someone to work customer service for your company. This person should be good at communicating with people and answering questions and should have the ability to work independently. They should be a good problem solver and have an even disposition.

Take your time. The person you hire must be someone you trust, because you will probably hire them to work independently doing tasks that you would normally be doing. You need to feel confident they can do it according your standards.

It is likely that, at least at first, you will be content with part-time staff. Very few eBay sellers actually have full-time employees, although there may come a time when it becomes necessary. Until that day, however, part-timers with flexible needs are best. The best scenario is to find someone, like a student or housewife/househusband, who just wants extra spending money and is not dependent on a paycheck to pay bills. With such an individual, you need not feel guilty when the work is slow and you do not need them to come in.

There will be seasonal times — like around Christmas — when you are doing more business, and may even need to have a full-time person, but only temporarily. You can often find people wanting full-time temporary work at universities. A student on winter break would be ideal for helping you with the Christmas rush.

Of course, do not overlook the possibility of using "casual labor" from your spouse or kids, who are much more likely to work for you just to help out and get a little extra spending money on an irregular basis. If you do employ family members, however, do not pay them "under the table," or you will risk losing track of your payroll expenses entirely and letting it go out of control. Even your own children should be paid with a legitimate paycheck, with taxes withheld, so you can have an audit trail and can legitimately deduct that expense from your own taxes.

You need to make sure that you do the taxes right for any employees, or even freelance labor. You might want to consider what you will be financially and legally responsible for if you decide to hire employees. You may need to check with the laws concerning hiring in your area and state. Make sure you follow the guidelines of fair hiring practices. A good place to look for and request copies of this information is from the United States Office of Personnel Management. They have the current laws and practices of hiring and maintaining employees at **www.opm.gov**.

If you have employees, make sure that you have a solid understanding of employee taxes, as these can be the trickiest taxes to have to deal with. If your company reaches a point where you feel that you should hire more employees, you need to be prepared to commit 30 percent of your payroll to taxes and paperwork. It will be your responsibility to withhold all your full- or part-time employees' federal and state income tax, Social Security, and Medicare taxes from paychecks. At tax time, you will need to remit them with your overall tax bill. In addition, you will have to pay your company's portion of Social Security and Medicare benefit funds. You must consider that employee salaries of up to $87,922 will likely be taxed 6.2 percent for Social Security and 1.45 percent for Medicare.

Social Security and Medicare taxes pay for benefits that workers and families receive under the Federal Insurance Contributions Act (FICA). Social Security tax pays for benefits under the old age, survivors, and disability insurance part of FICA. Medicare tax pays for benefits under the hospital insurance part of FICA. You have to pay your portion of your employees' taxes that matches what you have withheld from them. You should use Forms 941 to file the federal, Social Security, and Medicare taxes.

In addition to these taxes, you will also be responsible for Federal Unemployment Tax Act (FUTA) taxes. You have to pay this separately from other taxes. Your employees do not pay into this tax; you are totally responsible for it. This is another thing to consider before hiring others. You will need to file a form 940 to cover the FUTA taxes. Make sure that you deposit the taxes in a financial institution that is able to hold these types of funds.

Here is the calendar of when payroll taxes are due:

- April 30 for wages paid January – March
- July 31 for April – June
- October 31 for July – September
- January 31 for October – December

If you owe more taxes than $500, your due date changes to the fifteenth day of the next month.

There is another option you may want to consider instead of hiring employees, and that is hiring independent contractors. Hiring independent contractors can save you paperwork and expenses. If you hire seasonally, you will be more likely to hire these types of workers, as you need the extra help certain times of the year. A list of independent contractors is a good thing to develop.

The definition of independent worker applies to workers who are in business for themselves, and pay their own taxes and insurance. Independent workers will use their own equipment or facilities. One of the benefits of hiring independent contractors is that they require little or no supervision, and they are typically paid per day or for short periods of time. These are some things you must consider when determining whether a worker is an employee or an independent contractor. This assists you in avoiding the threat of tax fraud and liability charges. You must make sure that the above factors apply to them and that these points are clear to the workers.

One of the best ways to ensure that you do not make any errors in using independent contractors is to develop and use a written independent contractor's agreement. You can find a copy of it on the CD-ROM. Include the contractor's full name, address, and Social Security or EIN.

A bonus of using an independent contractor is that you do not have to withhold or pay any taxes on payment you make to them. They are responsible for their own taxes. A gauge that is generally used with an independent contractor is that the person for whom the services are performed has the right to control or direct only the result of the work and not what will be done and how it will be done or the method of accomplishing the result.

If you decide to hire a full-time or part-time employee, you may want them to sign a contract. A sample employment contract follows. This is in addition to them filling out a W-4 and state tax forms.

General Employment Contract

This Contract is made on ____________________, 20 ____ , between ______________________, Employer, of ____________________, City of ____________________, State of ______________________, and ______________________, Employee, of ______________________,
City of ______________________, State of ____________________.

In order for both parties to work together as a team, the Employer and Employee agree as follows:

1. The Employee agrees to perform the following duties and job description: *(Write down every aspect of the job the person is to do. If you add items later, they should be added on this form and initialed, or a new form should be created.)*

This is considered a full/part-time position. *(Circle one.)*

2. The Employee will begin work on ____________________, 20 ____. This position shall continue for a period of ____________________. *(Either a time frame or until a specific date.)*

3. The Employee will be paid the following:

Weekly salary: *(This may be hourly, monthly, or per event.)*

The Employee will also be given the following benefits: *(This may not be applicable, but follow state and federal guidelines concerning benefits.)*

Sick Pay:
Vacations:
Bonuses:
Retirement Benefits:
Insurance Benefits:

4. The Employee agrees to abide by all rules and regulations of the Employer at all times while employed. In addition, they will read and agree to the company's business plan, vision statement, and value statement.

5. This Contract may be terminated by:

(a) Breach of this Contract by the Employee
(b) The expiration of this Contract without renewal
(c) Death of the Employee
(d) Incapacitation of the Employee for over _______ days in any one year. *(You may choose to add, delete, or modify anything you choose in this section.)*

6. The Employee agrees to sign the following additional documents as a condition of obtaining employment: *(You can add other documents, such as a non compete agreement and an agreement not to divulge anything about the company and how it operates to any outside entity.)*

7. Any dispute between the Employer and Employee related to this Contract will be settled by voluntary mediation. If mediation is unsuccessful, the dispute will be settled by binding arbitration using an arbitrator of the American Arbitration Association. *(This is a professional organization that can help settle disputes outside of court for a fee. More information can be found at **http://www.adr.org/**.)*

8. Any additional terms of this Contract:

9. No modification of this Contract will be effective unless it is in writing and is signed by both the Employer and Employee. This Contract binds and benefits both parties and any successors. Time is of the essence of this Contract. This document is the entire agreement between the parties. This Contract is governed by the laws of the State of ____________________.

Dated:

____
Signature of Employer

____
Printed name of Employer

____
Signature of Employee

____
Printed name of Employee

(You may want to have a notary notarize your agreement)

You may also want to have a written contract with a particular company you are doing regular business with, such as a distributor or drop-shipper. It can save you money, time, and aggravation. If you ever have to take a company to court, having a signed contract can be the document to tip the scales in your favor. Following is a sample company agreement.

Company Agreement

This Agreement is made on ____________________, 20 ___, between
______________________________, Company (your eBay business), of ____________________,
City of ____________________, State of ____________________, and
______________________,
Hired Company (name of shipper or other business), of ____________________, City of
____________________, State of ____________________.

1. The (type of business), as an independent contractor, agrees to furnish all of the labor and materials to do the following portions of the work specified in the Agreement between the Company and the Hired Company (Shipper, etc.) dated ____________________, 20 ____.

2. The Hired Company agrees that the following portions of the total work will be completed by the dates specified:

Work:

Dates:

3. The Hired Company agrees to perform this work in a professional manner according to standard practices in their industry. If any plans or specifications are part of this job, they are attached to and are part of this Contract.

4. The Company agrees to pay the Hired Company as full payment
$ ____________________, for doing the work outlined above. This price will be paid to the Vendor on satisfactory completion of the work in the following manner and on the following dates:

Work:

Dates:

5. The Company and Hired Company may agree to extra services and work, but any such extras must be set out and agreed to in writing by both the Company and the Vendor.

6. The Hired Company agrees to indemnify and hold the Contractor harmless from any claims or liability arising from the Hired Company's work under this Agreement.

7. No modification of this Agreement will be effective unless it is in writing and is signed by both parties. This Agreement binds and benefits both parties and any successors. Time is of the essence of this Agreement. This document, including any attachments, is the entire agreement between the parties. This Agreement is governed by the laws of the State of
____________________.

Dated:

____
Signature of Company

____
Name of Company

____
Signature of Hired Company

____
Name of Hired Company

(You may want a notary to sign and seal this agreement)

Bonding

When you bond your business, you obtain a legal document that guarantees that you will complete the task your business promises as a condition of the terms of sale. Bonding is not the same as insurance. Bonds are underwritten to insure that the buyer is protected. In order for you to be bonded, you must make an application to a bonding company. They will prequalify you on the basis of credit history, performance, and character. Once a bond is granted, then the underwriter or surety company will guarantee to pay a buyer or replace an item if the seller fails to perform. If a seller does not meet the standards of their bonding agent, they can lose their bonded status.

Being bonded lets your buyers know that they can safely do business with you and that you are not some fly-by-night company. One of the companies that does bonding for eBay sellers is BuySafe, at **www.buysafe.com/seller_solutions/overview.html**. The site claims that being bonded can increase your sales by almost 15 percent.

Storage/Office Space

You will probably start out working out of your home. If you have a spare room that you can dedicate solely to your eBay business, so much the better. There are two advantages to this strategy. First, it is just easier to stay organized if you are not running your eBay business off your kitchen table, and you have some dedicated space for it. Second, you can probably qualify for the home-office deduction, which will save you some money on your taxes.

But there are circumstances where the home office will not work. Maybe you just do not have the space. Rather than renting an office space before your business can support it, the best strategy is just to hold off for as long as you can and try your best to keep your space organized. Get the outside office space as soon as you can, but do not do it prematurely.

If the biggest problem is storing goods, you may consider just renting a storage space instead of office space, which is likely to be much cheaper. If you do find that renting an office is absolutely necessary, you can still cut costs there by sharing space, or perhaps subletting part of an office from another company. It is common for larger companies to have rooms they are not using and are willing to sublet. Alternately, if you are enterprising and interested in real estate, you may consider buying an inexpensive yet large house and converting it into office space, taking the space you need and renting out the rest to cover your payments. Ideally, you would break even, or maybe make a small profit on the deal.

CHAPTER 10

Going Beyond eBay

Tips from the Experts

Start out with just eBay, but quickly transition into multiple income streams through information products, your own Web sites, consulting with small businesses about their online marketing, training others, growing your mailing list, etc. Any or all of those activities are a great way to hedge your bets and create multiple income streams.

— Jim Cockrum

Up-selling and cross-selling are not for amateurs. This chapter is for those who want to make good money and earn the title of "PowerSeller," and more importantly, "successful business person." The techniques presented here are not difficult to understand, but I suggest you reread the material a few times to totally digest it all.

Cross-selling and up-selling are the fine arts of convincing your customers to spend more than they originally intended. Your best customer is always going to be an existing one. It is easier to make a sale to somebody who has already bought something from you, or is in the process of buying something from you, which is why these two sales techniques are so vitally important.

Cross-selling occurs when your customer is buying one item, and you then offer something that complements what they are already buying. Up-selling occurs when your customer is buying one item and you offer them an opportunity to upgrade to a higher quality item of the same type.

One of the simplest examples of cross-selling occurs when you go into a fast food restaurant and the employee behind the counter asks, "Do you want fries with that?" Up-selling is when you walk into the same restaurant, and the employee asks, "Do you want to super-size that?" You walk away with the extra-huge soft drink and a bucket of fries, and you leave a little more money behind than you had intended.

It is a little different using these techniques online, but it can be done. There are two times when you can engage in these practices: before the sale and after the sale. The most successful PowerSellers often use these techniques.

Advantages of Cross-Selling

Simply put, cross-selling makes you more money. The environment of retail, especially online retail, is extremely competitive, and customers do not tend to be loyal to individual retailers. The very nature of eBay and Internet commerce is to allow shoppers to compare prices and products from different vendors. When most shoppers go to eBay, they do not go immediately to a certain eBay store. Rather, they go to the eBay search engine, input the name of the product they are looking for, and probably get a list of several dozen eBay stores.

This technology makes things easier for shoppers to find the best product at the best price, but it discourages customer loyalty. However, you can mitigate that loss of loyalty with several techniques, including cross-selling and up-selling.

After they have made a purchase, follow-up e-mails and newsletters will drive some return business, but you will get most of those extra sales in the immediate cross-sell at the time of sale.

Get them while they are in shopping mode. They have already decided to buy one item. Therefore, offer them something that goes with it right away. Your chances of selling two items in the same sale are greater than your chances of selling two items in two separate transactions.

Market research will also show that new customer acquisition is a time-consuming, and often costly, process, which is why it is important to maximize the revenue you gain from each sale. In the telecom industry, for example, carriers have recently started offering "bundles" of products to maximize the average revenue per user (ARPU). Instead of just buying phone service alone, you can now buy a bundle of phone service, Internet service, and cable television service, all at once.

Preparing the Cross-Sell

A big part of the cross-sell opportunity takes place before you even list the item. It takes place when you are acquiring your goods to sell. When you are searching out products, whether it is at yard sales, auctions, estate sales, or from wholesalers, finding the perfect product is only half the battle. Once you have found that good buy, that spectacular item you are sure will sell immediately at a high profit, start looking around for other things to go with it. You will always have better luck when you are selling several items in the same category, as opposed to just a random collection of "stuff."

Work Your Magic Before the Sale

Before you make the sale, prepare your auction site for possible cross-sell and up-sell by arranging your eBay store the right way. Group your products together in similar categories so that people will see the possibilities while they are browsing. There are two parts to this type of organization. First, you will create a main page with pictures of several products, and these products will be grouped together with photos of companion products situated adjacent to each other.

Second, when the shopper clicks on a given picture, you will have created a separate product page for each item, and when they click on the picture on the main page, they will be taken to this separate product page. On that separate product page, you will, of course, include a larger picture of the item with multiple views and a well-written description, but do not stop there. On that separate product page, somewhere near the bottom, also include a teaser about companion items. For example, if the product page is about an alligator-skin handbag, on the bottom, advertise your alligator shoes. Include a smaller picture of the shoes (your cross-sell), with a few lines, like, "What goes great with this beautiful alligator handbag? Matching shoes, of course, and we have them. Click on the picture to find out more."

Top Off Your Sale

After the sale, most eBay guides will tell you the standard protocol, which is to contact the winning bidder, restate the amount of the bid and payment options, ship the product, and ask for positive feedback. That is all fine, but that is not all.

There are automatic e-mailers that will send out automatic e-mail responses to notify bidders of their winning bid, but these automatic e-mails stop short of including an additional sales pitch and miss the mark. You lose a good marketing opportunity by limiting your follow-up to a simple, automated, procedural e-mail.

Instead, make your follow-up e-mail more personal. In addition to the necessary information, greet the buyer personally, and include a short, friendly message that tells about other products you have that would go well with what they just bought.

Go Beyond eBay

PowerSellers are selling goods outside of eBay. Maybe you have a separate e-commerce site where you sell other goods, or you list on other auctions. Maybe you even have a brick-and-mortar store. Do not hesitate to let your customers know, both in your follow-up e-mail and in subsequent marketing e-mails, where they can find your other offerings.

Accessories

Needless to say, accessories are a good business. If you sell computers, for example, there are many accessories that go with the computer, and you should carry a large, varied supply. If you want to sell used computers, you should also sell used printers, scanners, mice, glare screens, mouse pads, computer books, and other types of peripherals.

There are two approaches that you can take with accessories, and both work well. You can sell all the accessories separately, but make sure that they are readily accessible and visible from the main page. Do not hide them two or three levels deep. When a shopper clicks on that picture of your used PC, make sure the product page also has information and links to the various accessories they may want or need. Alternatively, you can combine the main product with two or three commonly used accessories for a larger primary sale.

There is Life Beyond eBay

While eBay may be a good tool for selling products, it is not the only one. The most successful entrepreneurs, and even PowerSellers, never rely on a single venue, but instead sell their products through multiple sites, including other auction sites, online malls, and SEO-optimized Web sites. These other venues can be used either to make additional sales directly or to drive traffic to your eBay store.

More than a store, eBay is a good tool that you use in your e-commerce initiatives to help you sell things. But you should not limit yourself only to one tool. There are more tools out there that you can use in your business, and they will help you become much more successful in the end. Like the carpenter's tools, each tool in your own retail toolbox will help you do different things.

Fortunately for you, you do not have to do all the cross-selling manually. There is a tool for you on eBay. When you view an item for sale, there is usually a small strip at the bottom of the page with a caption that reads something like, "See more great items from this seller." The strip then includes pictures of other items with links to those items.

This automatic cross-promote can be useful or useless, depending on how you approach it. If you just let the eBay tool randomly select the other items to view, chances are, you will not get a high degree of cross-sell. If you are featuring a purse, and the four cross-promoting items that appear on the bottom of the handbag feature page are a power drill, screwdriver set, hunting cap, and moustache trimmer, you probably are not going to get many clicks on those items.

You have to turn on this option in your "My eBay Preferences" page. Go to that page, click on "Participate in eBay Merchandising," and select "Cross Promote My Items." There are several different options to choose from. For example, you may decide to show items by when auctions end, showing the items for which bidding ends soonest. You can show the highest-priced items or just show "Buy It Now" items.

The eBay dialogue will then give you several options to design your cross promotion, and you can choose from several defaults. If all your items are similar, and in the same general category, you can simply choose to "Show Any Item," and eBay will just rotate items at random in the cross-promote section. In the first dialogue, you will select "Selling Format," "Gallery Items," and "Show My Items Sorted By." Then, you can select what products will show up with individual items, if you choose to do so.

However, if you are like many eBay sellers, you have items from several different categories, and you will have some products that just naturally go together. If you sell a coffee grinder, feature the gourmet coffee bean package in your cross-promotion strip.

The Online Auction Business

When you think of an online auction, chances are, you think of eBay first, as it is by far the largest. However, eBay is not the only one. Online auctions are big business, and there are other generalized auction venues like eBay, as well as more specialized ones that focus on particular product types, such as antique auctions or auctions for business services.

You may have made some good money on eBay, and you may have a certain sense of loyalty to the company, but that should not mean that you should restrict yourself. Branching out into other online auction venues may expand your business significantly. Even if eBay remains your largest producer, having two or three smaller-producing auction sites can go a long way toward helping you achieve a financial goal. In the world of business, more is usually better.

There are some good arguments for diversifying into other online auctions. While you should not give up on eBay entirely, there are some other auctions that may be more specialized and may be well-suited to a particular product line that you carry. A specialized auction site will have more savvy shoppers who are familiar with the real value of what you are offering. And while everybody loves a bargain, no matter where they are shopping, you are less likely to have your site bombarded by bargain-hunters who want to buy your $1,000 first edition book for $1.50.

Alternative Auction Sites

Amazon.com

You do not have to be a big publishing company to sell things on Amazon. It has, in fact, become a popular place for small-time book dealers to sell second-hand and rare books. It is not an auction site exactly. Instead, you are able to list your items for a fixed price. We usually associate Amazon with discount items, and that was how it first got started in the business — as a large online book dealer. But today, you can buy and sell just about anything on **Amazon.com**.

It is easy to get started on Amazon.com as a seller, and you will notice on the home page that there is a sidebar that says "selling on Amazon." The links under this will take you to an information page that tells you everything you need to know. As with eBay, you also make a description of the product you have to sell, set a price, and register with Amazon Payments so you can collect your money.

There is a closing fee that varies, a per-transaction fee of 99 cents, plus a percentage of the sales price. The good news is that you get 60 days worth of listing time, and if the item does not sell, you do not have to pay anything. If you do not just want to sell a few odd items, you can become a Pro Merchant.

Pro Merchant listings do not close after 60 days, and you save a little money on listing fees, since Pro Merchants do not have to pay the 99 cent listing fee. Also, just as on eBay, you can create your own online shop on **Amazon.com**.

Overstock.com

Overstock.com offers sellers a chance to sell their products at a discount to wholesale price. They evaluate your items and decide whether you can sell through them or not. They check the prices you are offering to sell your items for compared to other sellers, but once a price is decided on, you are locked in.

Webidz.com

Webidz.com is a similar site to eBay and is growing daily. The good thing about this site is that there are no fees to list before or after the sale of an item. There are add-on features that do cost a fee, but the basic selling of an item is absolutely free. It is a good place to try to sell unsold items you had listed on eBay. The site works similar to eBay, and the auctions look similar as well.

Epier.com

Epier.com is almost the same as Webidz, except they do have a closing fee like eBay that is based upon how much the item sold for. They also have bigger packages that you can buy, much the same as eBay.

Bid-alot.com

Bid-alot.com has been on the scene since 2003 and offers a $2 a month membership fee. There are no closing costs or insertion costs. It costs an additional $2 registration fee and $2 a month store-front fee. They also offer other slightly more expensive packages and add-ons.

Sell Online Direct

An auction site, whether it is eBay or one of the others, does not have to be your primary means of sales. Many vendors have much success creating their own e-commerce Web sites and offering products for sale directly. Your own site can be a wonderful supplement to your eBay presence, and you can establish a two-way referral between your eBay store and your own e-commerce store.

The best strategy is to use your own e-commerce storefront to sell other items that are not in your eBay store, but are in the same general category. That way, you will continue to get cross-traffic, as people look for more items as they shop. Another advantage is that if you are running your own storefront, you are not paying anybody any listing fees, and you can list a product there indefinitely. It is good for listing products that have not sold on eBay. After one relisting on eBay, unless it is a highly unusual, expensive item, it is usually time to give it up. The cost of three listings on eBay for any given product is probably going to eat your profits, and then it is time to move that product to one of the free auction sites, or in this case, to your own e-commerce storefront site.

There are several different ways to create your own e-commerce site, and there are plenty of ready-made templates available that make the set-up easy. There is a little more involved here than just listing a product on an auction site, since you have to take care of everything yourself, including the back-end financials. You have to set up a method of accepting credit card payments.

Setting up your own e-commerce Web site takes a few steps. As there have been several books written about the subject, we will not attempt to get into all the details here. But briefly, here is what is involved:

1. Get a credit card merchant account or use a service
2. Obtain hosting space (usually inexpensive)
3. Create your Web site, from scratch or using a template
4. List your site on all the major search engines
5. Cross-promote your site with your other online presences

Festivals, Fairs, and Flea Markets

While festivals, fairs, and flea markets are quite a departure from selling online, they are worth considering. Some vendors make big money at these events. You register, pay a fee, set up a table, and display your products.

This avenue can be a good adjunct to your eBay business, and a good way to promote it. These events are often quite crowded. Thousands of people may walk by your table in a day. You will naturally make some sales, but perhaps more important, you can direct people to your eBay business. There will be plenty of people who like what you have displayed, but do not want to buy that day, are short on cash, or just cannot make up their minds. Directing them to your eBay site will give them an option other than waiting until the next festival to see you again.

Have a stack of brochures, fliers, or attractive post cards with a picture of your goods on them, and give these out liberally to everyone who stops, or even pauses, in front of your table. This printed material should give a brief description of your business, have contact information, and provide the URL of your eBay store and any other online presences you may have. In addition, create a large sign that can be seen from a distance, saying something to the effect of "Visit me online at eBay!" Doing so not only encourages passers-by to check you out online, it also lends you a bit of instant credibility. Shoppers at the festival will recognize eBay and will know instantly that you are not just a hobbyist. You are a PowerSeller.

CHAPTER 11

Advertise, Advertise, Advertise

If you were starting a traditional business in your hometown, there are numerous things you would do to spread the word, but placing an ad in your local newspaper is not going to get the word out to 135 million people worldwide.

There are many ways to make yourself more visible on eBay. Even small things can make a difference, so consider using all the resources you have available at little or no cost to you.

Let's take a brief look at the free marketing strategies you should be employing. These five free ways to make your listings stand out are available to every eBay seller.

Cross-Promotions

This is the box at the bottom of your listing that says "Other Great Items From This Seller," and it does not cost you anything to have it. To get it, go to your "My eBay" page and click on "Marketing Tools" (under "My Account") and click the link that says "Promoting Similar Items." Edit your promotion preferences here. If you are using all the cross-promotions available, it will say "Participate in cross-promotions" and then "Yes in all available areas" after that. That is it, and you have free help from eBay to drive lookers and buyers to all your other listings and your store, as a link to your store is placed in that box as well.

Some of the places that your cross-promotions will be displayed include the e-mails sent to non-winning bidders letting them know they did not win the auction. When someone places your item on their "Items I am Watching" page, they will see some of your other cross-promoted items as well. Even when a buyer pays an invoice through PayPal, they will again be shown a choice of items that they can purchase from you.

Check Out My Other Listings

Even though eBay puts up a nifty box of your other auctions, it is at the bottom of the auction page, and sometimes, it just does not get noticed. While you are writing out your auction text, add a link to your other listings.

Cross-Promotion Connections

You can make arrangements with other sellers to promote each other's items. This is good if you sell widgets, but not the specialty cleaner that keeps your widget looking new. Cross-promote with the sellers who sell complementary items, not competing items. Check out the information under "My Account" and "Marketing Tools."

"About Me" Page

Every eBay member has the opportunity to create an "About Me" page at no cost to them. Some people post pictures of pets, local tourist attractions, or themselves, giving their customers a "face." Others are more business-like, sharing information about their merchandise or customer-service philosophy. If you have not yet made your "About Me" page, do so soon.

To create your page, go to "Community," on the top toolbar, and scroll to the bottom of the page, where you will see the link, "Create an About Me Page," inviting you to create a page. The step-by-step instructions walk you through a series of boxes where you type in your text, make your choices, and preview your page.

You can use your own HTML, if you are lucky enough to know that already. Enter your HTML simply by clicking on the "HTML" tab. If you are like many new sellers, and have not been exposed to much HTML yet, all you have to do is use the drop-down menus to choose your font type, size, and color. The buttons for bold, italic, underline, numbering, bullets, and more are all pretty standard; they should look just like those in any word-processing software you use. Spend a little time making your page interesting to look at. Do not use a font that is too small, or too large, as it will appear as though you are shouting. Use different colors for the different sections, such as personal information, business information, policies, and customer service.

You can also link to photos that you have stored online or your company's logo, if you have one already. Even if you just put up some basic information, at least it is a start. Surf around eBay and look at other sellers' pages (there is no way to search "About Me" pages; you need to just click on the "me" logo after any seller's name you encounter on the site) to get ideas for your own page, but do not steal any logos or photos.

Personal information should be friendly and interesting, but perhaps not too personal. You do not want to offend potential customers by stating any views on controversial topics. Additionally, for security reasons, it may not be wise to get too detailed about where you live or the identity of other family members, especially any minors who live in your home.

Pets, however, are a good thing to talk about and share photos of. Also, your travels, the seasonal scenery in your part of the country, or a photo of your workshop might be appropriate. If you make your product by hand, show an item in different stages of completion, and perhaps a description of how the item is made with care and attention to details.

Business information you might want to share could include your mission statement from your business plan and your customer-service philosophy. If you have not yet put one to paper, now is a good time to do so. Your statement might read something like this:

Our goal is to serve all our customers in a timely manner with fair prices, speedy delivery, and service after the sale! We want to make every customer a repeat customer. If there's anything about our service that you feel needs improvement, feel free to e-mail me personally at WillysWidgets@e-mailprovider.com.

If your product has any exemplary features or has won any awards, praise, or good reviews, cite these, and the source that you got this information from, as well. For example:

Our widgets are made by the finest facility in North America. The Widget Review (July 2008) states that "these widgets outperform every other model on the market. You can't go wrong when you invest in this easy-to-maintain and quiet-running model!"

You will also need to choose whether you want any current items listed to appear after your text. You can even choose how many items you want to provide links to. Additionally, you can have your last ten, twenty, or more feedback listings displayed, with a link inviting the reader to go to your member profile and view all your feedback. Good feedback is something that sellers are proud of, and you should always take the opportunity to share your well-deserved feedback rating.

You will also be able to insert links to Web sites, including your own company's site, with certain restrictions that are clearly laid out (click the link on the "About Me" creation page), and HTML images. To further personalize your page, you can choose from one of three layouts, and then preview your information in the chosen layout. If you want to see the other layouts, simply go back and choose again.

Editing your page follows the same process. To edit your page, go to the page and scroll to the bottom. There, you will find a link directing you through the editing process. Keep your page current, and edit it anytime you have a new product line or announcement to make about your business. Also, try changing the photos seasonally to help those looking at the page know it is current.

When your page is complete, eBay will provide you with a link to your new "About Me" page, which you should make a point of writing down. Add it to your e-mail templates or signature so that every business e-mail you send points prospective customers to your page, which highlights your product and your feedback.

Linking to and from eBay

Promote your eBay store, your "About Me" page, and auctions on other Web sites via your e-mail. In addition to using your "About Me" page link, you will be able to link people directly from their e-mail to your store when the e-mail is opened. When you link from your "About Me" page, make sure you are within the requirements of eBay's policy; linking from your "About Me" page to your own personal Web site or domain name is important.

You cannot link from your "About Me" page to another auction site that you also may sell on; it must be to your own personal Web page. However, on that Web page, you can link to other sites you auction on as well. Check out eBay's policies thoroughly before linking; you do not want to offend the company who is helping your business get a good running start. Linking is an important part of Internet marketing via e-mail and message boards, which are also considered "free" marketing techniques.

Internet Chat Rooms

Internet chat rooms and message boards can also be a way to spread the word about your eBay business. Check around for eBay-related sites that are not affiliated with eBay. There are dozens of Yahoo! Groups devoted to eBay, some of which exist only for members to post their listings, specials, and links to their store. There is no cost involved to you; just a few minutes of your time to post the information. Try looking for message boards and chat rooms devoted to your particular product, as you will probably not generate much interest in your heavy metal music sales if you are posting ads on a board of senior citizens who are looking to buy travel-related products.

These suggestions are not all-encompassing. Check out the eBay "Community" discussion boards on the topic of free marketing, where you can learn some tricks of the trade without having to figure them out the hard way.

Few businesses can survive solely on the free marketing they can do. While it is important to use every possible opportunity you get to advertise your business for free, you will probably have to pay for some services as well. Let's look at some marketing ideas that are worth paying for.

As with the free marketing ideas listed above, we will begin by looking at the for-a-fee services that eBay offers first. It only makes sense that if you are using eBay as your primary selling tool, you will also use every possible option eBay has to market your business and products.

eBay Stores

Probably one of the most common tools used by sellers is the eBay Store. The fees for having your own eBay store are reasonable, if you were to compare the price for renting a traditional store space or regularly placing ads in the local newspaper. Once you are a registered eBay seller, and have earned a feedback score of 20, you are eligible to open a store.

eBay suggests that you open a store when you are ready to sell regularly. This is not a good choice for the occasional seller, because there are ongoing fees. Also, you should have sufficient inventory and a regular product stream set up. The basic eBay store can be had for just $15.95 per month, with the first 30 days at no cost to you. The benefits of having your own eBay store are numerous, including:

- A professional presence on eBay that says "I'm a PowerSeller"
- Lower listing fees for store inventory items
- Longer listing times (or never-ending listings) for store inventory
- The ability to categorize your merchandise how you choose
- Five pages in your store
- A place to showcase all your listings, including current auctions
- Free Selling Manager software use
- Cross-promotions in more places for store sellers
- The ability to link a domain name directly to your store
- Final Value Fee credits if your off-eBay referral buys from your store inventory
- Accounting Assistant (software that works with QuickBooks)
- Free e-mail marketing tools
- Sales reports for your store and other listings
- Special features for upgraded store types (Featured and Anchor Stores)

An online presence is crucial, and a permanent storefront is one way to achieve it. Whether you have the basic or the Anchor Store, you can use eBay's tools — or your own HTML — to create an attractive store that showcases your merchandise. It takes time to set up a store that "looks" zippy and professional, but if you take the time to read all the associated help files and use the built-in tools, you will soon have an attractive store that will be not just look like another auction listing page.

Your store will show all your current listings, whether they are fixed-price listings, auctions, or "store inventory" listings, which are sold through "Buy It Now" only. Now you must decide what to put into inventory and what to auction.

There are differing theories about this, and it will depend on your product. If you sell primarily the same products repeatedly, then you should always run some auctions, because when lookers do a search from the home page (at the top right), they will see auctions, including fixed-price listings, in their results, not store inventory.

If a looker's search turns up 30 or fewer results, then up to 30 store inventory listings will appear after the auction listings. If the search turns up more than 30 results, then there will be a link at the bottom of the page letting buyers know that the same items can be located in eBay stores. All they have to do is click to be taken to a page of store listings.

If a search turns up no auction or fixed-price listings matching the searcher's criteria, but there are store inventory items that match, then up to 30 of the store inventory items will be displayed with a gallery photo. A gallery photo is different than a regular photo in that is displayed when you click on the green camera icon. Gallery photos are the photos that a buyer sees when they are browsing search results. You must pay a little extra for the gallery photo.

The difference between a fixed-price auction and a store inventory item is primarily the number of days that it is available for sale. Fixed-price auctions run the same as regular auctions, for one, three, five, seven, or ten days only. In your store, you will be able to set up your inventory items to be for sale for 30, 60, 90, or 120 days, or for as long as you like, or until you cancel it. You can convert any store inventory item back to an auction item at any time, if you wish.

Listings that never expire are for items that you always stock or always produce. But do not start mentally adding up the listing fees just yet; when you list store inventory items, the listing price is currently two cents for a whole 30 days. The Final Value Fees are higher for store inventory items, though.

Do not forget that your store will not get the same type of exposure as auctions in the buyer's basic search — there is no way for buyers to specify that they want to search store inventory only or in addition to auctions — so you would be wise to still run auctions. Think of them as a tool to drive people to your store.

Not to say that stores are entirely without their own promotion. Your store will be listed in the directory of all stores, which can be easily accessed from the home page. Some people prefer to buy from a store rather than wait it out in an auction, so they search by going to the "eBay Stores" page first.

On the eBay Stores page, the buyer can search by store names or by matching items. If a buyer wants to find out who is selling gidgets in an eBay store, they can search "gidget," and the search will return a list of stores that currently list a gidget in their inventory. This is the only place on eBay that lookers can go to search specifically in stores' inventory.

But do not rely on buyers always doing a search on the "eBay Stores" page; write a sentence or two that you will always include in every auction text, suggesting that the looker could find much more variety and choice in your store. Save your text in a word-processing program, insert it into every auction, and make sure to put it in your Turbo Lister templates. The point is to get lookers to check out your store, even if they are not as interested in the auction item once they have seen it.

There are three different types of eBay stores to choose from. Below I have listed the types, the cost, and brief descriptions of each type of store. You can find the most up-to-date information at **http://pages.eBay.com/storefronts/SubscriptionGuide.html**.

Basic

- 15.95/month
- Sell at least 10 items/$100 per month
- For a secondary income or hobby
- Able to use Selling Manager for free
- Limited space, e-mails, and customer service

Premium

- 49.95/month
- Most common type used by a PowerSeller
- Sell at least fifty items/$500 per month
- 24/7 customer service
- Able to use Selling Manager Pro for free
- More e-mails and listings you can manage
- More space for photos

Anchor

- 299.95/month
- Sell at least 500 items/$5,000 per month
- All of the features of Premium with increased space for pages and photos
- Store name frequently appears in "Shop eBay Stores" area of matching search results

Remember that your buyers will not know which type of service that you have. It is up to you to customize your store and make it look professional while making it easy for buyers to browse through. Here are some areas to pay attention to, as you can change and modify them according to you and your buyers' needs:

- You can change the store design. This includes the name, theme, gallery view, and the order that your items are sorted in.
- You can customize your pages. You should have a policies page that answers questions about your policies, such as shipping and payment.
- You should make sure that it is clear where you will ship to and where you will not.
- If you are collecting sales tax, make sure you have this included on your policies page. This will depend on the state you are selling from and selling to.
- Include customer service and return policies. You should also include your contact information and when customer service is available; include what your time zone is.

- You can name up to 300 different custom categories that allow your buyers to browse in specific areas for items. This helps make your store unique based on the types of items that you have for sale.

- You can use promotion boxes on your eBay store that allows you to give your store a different look every month and when you are placing items on sale.

Domain Names

When you are a store seller, and your looker bids or buys, you also have cross-promotions presented to the bidder/buyer. Of course, one of the best ways to promote your eBay store is to get a domain name and then have it go straight to your eBay store when anybody on the Internet clicks on it. There are costs to having a domain name, but they are fairly reasonable, especially if you do not actually have a Web site there. Think of a domain name as a portal for now, with the potential to be yet another selling tool — an off-eBay Web site — in the future.

One good reason to get a domain name is that eBay will give you credits on final value fees on sales of your store inventory (not auctions, even though they, too, are listed in your store) if the buyer got to your store from outside eBay through your own marketing efforts. Therefore, that domain name you are considering can pay for itself if people use it to get to your store and then make a purchase. Be sure you understand eBay's policies on this so that you meet all the requirements properly.

PowerSelling Tip

When you have an eBay store, consider advertising it locally, the same way you would advertise a brick-and-mortar store, such as through the newspaper, the Yellow Pages, or radio ads. These may be especially effective if you also have a Web site address (domain name) to advertise along with it.

There are also four additional tools you will be able to use free when you open a store: Selling Manager, Accounting Assistant (works with QuickBooks), e-mail marketing, and Sales Reports.

Selling Manager

Selling Manager is a program that makes your "My eBay" page's "All Selling" tab slicker, more productive, and more useful. It is a strongly suggested selling tool for medium- and high-volume sellers. It usually costs $4.99 per month, but it comes with a free 30-day trial, so consider trying it for the 30 days before you open your store.

One of the nice features of this program is its ability to track your sales contacts. Selling Manager can help you with that e-mail database you are planning to keep. It also includes some nice e-mail templates, plus templates for invoices and shipping labels. You can even create templates for feedback comments that you can store and use for your customers.

This software will archive four months of your listings, unlike the standard in "My eBay," which shows only those listings for sixty days back. There is also a tool in there to help you download your selling history, which can be helpful for your bookkeeping. For those of you who set up your books in QuickBooks right away, Accounting Assistant will interface with QuickBooks to make all those tasks easier.

E-mail Marketing

E-mail marketing is crucial, and since you will have Selling Manager keeping track of all your sales contacts, you can use the free e-mail marketing techniques to send up to 100 e-mails monthly to your contacts if you have a basic store; upgraded levels get more. If you need to send more than 100 e-mails through this system, there is a 1-cent charge for each additional e-mail.

While this may not be a cost-effective way to send out thousands of e-mails a month (when you only have the basic store), take advantage of it, at least monthly, until your contact list reaches 100 buyers. eBay provides a step-by-step guide to help you set up your strategy and system.

Sales Reports

Sales reports are a good way to get a quick glimpse of your overall sales, the percentage of your sales that come from auctions versus store inventory, or the sales for each of your store's categories. The features and freebies of the basic store are excellent for the fee charged. Sellers who immerse themselves into their eBay selling and learn to use all the tools available to them (there are even more than what we were able to cover here) will never regret paying their eBay bill at the end of each month.

At some point, you will be successful enough to upgrade to a "Feature Store." The monthly fee is not unreasonable because you will have access to these additional benefits:

- Your store's name and brief description rotated among all feature stores and shown on the "eBay Stores" page in the center (not the top box, but the one below it)

- Up to ten pages that you can fully customize by category or price, a page for promotions/specials, a dedicated home page, and other pages

- The ability to minimize the eBay header on all your pages, giving you more room for your own information

- Traffic reports that give details about what buyers are looking at most, and from where they entered your store (i.e., your own domain, eBay, or another location)

- More detailed sales reports than with the basic store

- Your inventory listings are more likely to appear at the bottom of the page where a buyer searched for auctions with certain keywords

- $30 per month to use on eBay's keyword program

- Selling Manager Pro included free ($15.95/month value)

An "Anchor Store" will give you premium exposure and services on the "eBay Stores" home page, but this little venture will put you out close to $500 per month. This upgrade may be something to write down and post on your wall as a goal.

Keywords

The term "keyword" has two meanings in eBay lingo. The meanings are related, but must be differentiated or overall chaos can ensue. Let's start with the simple meaning for keyword.

When buyers search for listings, they type in words that they think might be in the title of something they want to purchase. If they are in the market for an expensive watch for Grandpa's retirement gift, they might type in "Rolex" or some other high-end brand name of watches. In that case, Rolex is the keyword that connected the buyer with Grandpa's new watch.

The second meaning for keyword is basically the same: a word or phrase that is searched. eBay allows sellers to bid on the right to have their store's advertising displayed when their chosen keyword is searched by buyers. If you perform a search for "Rolex watch," you will get auction listings for Rolexes, and just above the first auction listing, there are a couple of boxes that pop up, trying hard to entice you into clicking on them and checking out their Rolexes.

If you click on one of the boxes, you will likely be taken to that particular seller's store. This is how the higher-volume sellers who can afford more than the minimum advertising in their budget keep their merchandise at the top of the list. They also can then make a sale without having an auction at the top of the list, which, by default, shows auctions ending first.

Many PowerSellers swear by this technique, and when you have a Featured or Anchor Store, you will have an allocated amount of money to spend on the keywords program. You are only charged for your banner at the top of the page every time a customer clicks on it. So while your banner might display 15 times in a 24-hour period, you will only be charged the fee for the 2 times that it was used to enter your store.

You can also purchase keyword banners if you only have a basic store, but there is an upfront fee charged, in addition to the per-click fee. When you have your store set up, go to the "Manage My Store" link and click on "Purchase Keywords" to learn about the fees and restrictions.

The search engine Google has a keyword per-click program called AdWords. Once you start using keyword banner programs, and feel you have a sense of how to best use your keywords to drive business to your eBay store — or your domain name, which in turn drives customers to your eBay store — then check into this program as well, at **http://adwords.google.com/select/Login3**.

Off-eBay Web Sites

Your own domain name can be used without an actual Web site attached to it; it can be used as a stand-alone product that merely refers potential customers to your eBay store. But once you have the income and time to devote to setting up an off-eBay Web site and maintaining it, then you should look into getting your own Web site/store.

The cost can vary greatly depending on a number of factors, such as your ability to create the site, either yourself (using a software such as Microsoft FrontPage, Adobe GoLive, or Macromedia Dreamweaver) or with the help of a friend or family member.

If you prefer to hire someone, you may find big price differences when you check with several companies. Sometimes, small, in-home businesses will create sites cheaper than the "big guys." Just be sure you are getting the best Web site and hosting deal for your money, including features, such as a secure server with shopping cart. There are companies online that will design an original site for you as well, so do not limit yourself to local companies (although, keeping your business local may be something you like to do).

Your hosting company will also be able to submit your site to all the major search engines so that people can find the site when they search for words that are applicable. One good thing about Web site search engines is that they will also search the content of your site so that matching phrases and words will be shown, not just matches in your site's name.

Having your own Web site can lend itself to yet another new marketing opportunity: affiliated marketing. This is a method whereby you loan out space on your site to another company's banner, and in return, if customers go to the other site via your site, you get either a per-click fee or a percentage of the profits when the customer purchases something.

Affiliated marketing is popular and should be considered when you get to this level of sales and marketing. Be sure to check into having your banner ad on other Web sites as well.

You can use your Web site for a variety of purposes. You can conduct product sales on your site, in addition to conducting them from an eBay store. You can use your Web site as an information portal as well, merely providing information about your product and directing all sales back to your eBay store.

Willy might set up a Web site to sell his widgets and gidgets, without paying eBay fees to do so. But since he can earn some credit on his final value fees by directing his Web site traffic to his eBay store, he may also choose to focus on maintenance of his widget or showcasing the newest models of widgets and gidgets, which can be purchased in his eBay store. Either way, when potential buyers search the Internet for "widget," "gidget," or any other related word, they will be directed to Willy's site. These are just a few ways that you can add a Web site to your existing sales approach.

PowerSelling Tip

The point of having a memorable name and logo for your store is for people to easily recognize and remember it. Take the time to develop your business name and logo, as it can help boost your repeat sales and word-of-mouth advertising.

Business Cards

Spend the money to buy good stationary and business cards. Do not waste your time printing them out on a printer. Nothing says cheap and unprofessional like homemade business cards. That does not mean you have to spend a fortune having business cards made. You can have 100 cards printed for about $10. Have them printed on good, heavy-stock paper. You are trying to win people over with your style and panache, and that begins with your business card.

Having good stationary is important. You will be sending out thank-you cards and letters to vendors and clients often. Having stationary made of good-stock paper with your logo and information is classy.

Your business card should have the logo and business name prominently displayed. The contact information and your name should be in smaller type. Pick a color that is easy on the eye. If you choose a background, make it simple. The more things you put on a card, the harder it will be to read. Keep it simple.

In addition to business cards, you can order thousands of products with your company name, eBay store name, Web site address, or company logo on them. You can get everything from baseball caps and pens and pads of paper to small toys, all with your information on them.

Pass out these items to your family and friends, as well as at gatherings, such as parades (simply walk through the crowd; you do not have to be in the parade itself) and community gatherings (e.g., picnics, your child's tee ball game, school programs, or the county fair). Do not make a pest of yourself, but if you are excited about your product, your store, and your business, people will want to hear about it and pass the word along for you. You never know where your next customer will come from.

PowerSelling Tip

Novelty products bearing your company name are nice items to tuck into an order as a way to encourage your buyers to come back soon. You could also send along a business card with a message on the back, such as, "Pass this card on to a friend who will receive a 10 percent discount when placing an order," and then, when you get a customer who mentions having a card of yours, ask which customer gave it to them. You can send the referring customer a thank-you e-mail with an invitation for 10 percent off their next order as well.

Newspaper, Magazine, and Radio Ads

Other traditional advertising methods might serve a purpose for you, such as newspaper and radio advertising. If your product is heavily used or highly desirable in a particular geographic location or among specific populations — such as in warm climates, during the summertime, or college students — then consider ads in publications that will reach those audiences.

If your product is popular with college students, contact college newspapers, which often have reasonable rates and are starved for advertisers. Trade journals are a good place for ads if your product is applicable to one particular field, such as for use by medical professionals. Regional magazines that are published for a local readership may have good advertising rates, in addition to helping you target your audience in that region.

Local radio stations might also be willing to pursue an advertising campaign for you. Look into sponsoring a particular hour of the day, such as rush hour, when people stuck in their cars might be more likely to listen. Try offering a product as a "prize" once a day to "caller number five." Pay to have the station's deejays wear shirts and hats with your company logo at local functions, and pass out some of your giveaways to the crowd.

There are many ways radio stations can help you build your company's name locally, and while you may have only a small percentage of your sales locally, if everyone in your county knows about your company, they will be more likely to refer their friends and family to your site.

These ideas are just some of the ways that you can advertise your eBay business, ranging from the free to the frivolous. Name recognition is what it is all about; even if people cannot always remember your name or phone number, if you can implant your Web site address in their subconscious, you have succeeded.

Now that you have some ideas on where to obtain your merchandise and how to set up payment, shipping, and advertising plans, you are close to starting the actual business of selling. Let's look quickly at the differences between your old eBay status as a looker, buyer, or occasional seller and your new relationship with eBay as a serious seller.

Note: Fees for store inventory are based on duration, not quantity. See eBay's policies to gain a thorough understanding of store fees, as this is merely an overview.

Checklist of Tasks: Planning Your Advertising

- I have set up my eBay preferences to use cross-promotions effectively
- I have created my "About Me" page
- I have set up a place to securely store my customer database so that I can e-mail specials or newsletters to my customers
- I am aware of the benefits of opening an eBay store and will consider doing so when I have a regular product stream and the financial ability to move ahead
- I understand eBay's policies against keyword spamming and choose to be an ethical seller who will not engage in this behavior
- I understand that I can advertise on sites like Google for a per-click fee when my budget will allow me to do so
- I will consider a domain name, for the purpose of directing traffic to my eBay store, and ultimately to have as an ecommerce site, when I am financially able
- I will use common techniques, such as business cards, giveaways, and local advertising to help drive customers to my eBay business

Buy
Shift

CHAPTER 12

A Picture is Worth a Thousand Words

The next time you go to your favorite retail store, pay attention to what seems to draw you to products. Note how much thought must have gone into the placement of products and how they look. For instance, say we just stepped into Barnes and Noble, a major seller of books and textbooks. The first thing you see are tables covered with books stacked in orderly piles, with featured titles stood up so that you can see the book covers. All the shelves in front of the store are set up in a similar fashion. Most of those books are set up to have their covers facing you as soon as you enter the store.

Barnes and Noble operates like this because they understand the value of showcasing your products correctly. Nothing is more important for an online vendor than the words they use and the pictures they showcase. The taking and displaying of photos is going to be the focus of this chapter. Most online shoppers will not even look at an auction if there is no picture. At least if there is a picture, there can be some assurance that the desired product actually exists; it gives the customer something to sink their minds into. When they are considering whether they are going to buy your product, they will be using your text and, most importantly, your pictures to mentally examine your item and determine whether they are going to buy it.

Again, next time you are at the store, Barnes and Noble perhaps, notice how people decide whether they are going to buy a book: they hold it in their hand, turn it over, and may even read a couple of pages; in short, they are examining the item. If you properly use your pictures and text, you will allow your customers in the online environment to do the same.

Two Vital Ingredients

Two of the most important tools for taking quality pictures are a digital camera and image editing software. You do not need to buy the highest-grade camera and software, but there are guidelines you should follow when deciding what to buy.

Your Imaging Editing Software

For most of the things you need to do with your pictures, such as making them brighter, sharper, crisper, or for adding text, any basic editing software will do. Adobe Photoshop Elements is an excellent, relatively inexpensive software package that will cost you about $100. Also, look around on your computer, as you may have some prepackaged editing software that will do everything you would want to do with your photos. If you own a Mac, then you should already have iPhoto on your computer, which is a solid picture editing tool.

Your Digital Camera

- **Digital cameras only**. Make sure it is a digital camera. While film cameras have their own advantages, for marketing your products online, a digital camera is a necessity. That way, you will not have to pay to get a picture developed before scanning it into your computer. All you will have to do is plug your camera into your computer and upload the photos.

- **Use folders and name your photos**. Keep your photos organized in folders so they can be easily found when needed. Also, refrain from using the computer-generated name for your photos, which should look something like "S7300572_2.JPG." Take the time as you upload photos to give them easily recognizable names, like IronPot1 and IronPot2, for example. That way, you will easily be able to keep track of your photos.

- **Megapixels matter**. When it comes to picture quality, megapixels matter. One megapixel stands for one million pixels. And a single pixel is short for one picture element, or a single point in a graphic image. Pixels work together like pieces of a jigsaw puzzle to make up a picture. The more pixels that make up a picture, the higher the quality of the photo. For larger objects, such as buildings, people, or cars, you can get away with a camera with a lower megapixel rating, such as 2.0 to 4.0 megapixels. Though, for smaller items, such as jewelry or decorative pins, you are going to need something with a higher megapixel rating, preferably 5.0 or higher. Commonly, the price of cameras increases as the megapixels increase, but shop around. With today's advances in microelectronics, it is getting cheaper to produce higher megapixel cameras, so you can easily find a good quality camera for less than $200.

- **Do not use a digital zoom**. Try to purchase a camera that zooms in using an actual lens attachment. If the camera says "digital zoom," it is fine for recreational use, and you may be able to get away with using it for some of your products, but to make certain your pictures are always of the highest quality, make sure you are not using a digital zoom. A digital zoom is not actually zooming in on the subject, but is using extrapolating software to rebuild what the subject would look like if it were closer. Using this type of zoom decreases the amount of megapixels in your photo, and consequently, your picture will be of poorer quality.

Some Useful Extras

Besides the camera and the editing software, you are going to want to invest in some extras. Not all these extras need to be purchased at once. Depending on what you are selling, you may want to get some of them right away. Other items can stay on your "wish list" and be used as business purchases to help lower the amount of taxes you will owe at the end of the year.

- **Props**. Some props that can help you take good quality photos are some plain black and white cloth to use as a backdrop for photos and some type of specialized displays. For example, if you are selling necklaces, you will want some type of jewelry display, which will make it look much better than just laying it flat. As a rule, props should be used but kept to a minimum, so as not to distract from the product.

- **Fixed tripod**. A tripod will take the concentration out of having a steady hand and make lining up your photos a snap. This is an excellent investment because it will help you take high-quality pictures more consistently and effortlessly.

- **Lenses**. Besides megapixels, nothing can affect the total quality of your picture more than a good lens. A fully functional close-up lens will bring out all those extra features that you are going to want your customer to be able to see. Do some research and find out what types of lenses you should invest in for your camera.

- **Lighting**. Make sure you have good lighting for your photos. At first, you are going to have to experiment to get the lighting just right. Professional photographers have a whole slew of tools that they use to get their lighting just right. Although you may want to acquire some of these eventually, to begin with, all you are likely to need are a couple of extra lamps.

- **Scanner**. Even though you will be mostly uploading images from your digital camera, a scanner is good to have, just in case. For pages of books, old comics, posters, and other flat objects, a scanner is ideal. It is also good to have if you need to take an image of a paper document to send in an e-mail. As an added bonus, most scanners and printers come with their own image editing software.

- **Clothing stands and mannequins**. If you sell clothes, they are going to look much better displayed on a model than just folded or laid flat. Also, with some minor editing, you can make almost anybody look like a model, so if you have someone who looks good in clothes and is willing, use them.

Advanced Lighting

The following is a list of some professional photography gear that will vastly increase your picture quality, and it will make taking quality pictures a snap. Yet, they are a serious investment, and most likely, you will not be able to purchase everything at once. For your purposes, the items already mentioned may be enough, but for the serious photographers out there, here are some ideas:

- A Cloud dome spreads out the light from your camera's flash, which reduces the white spot on the item and evens out the rest of the light from the room.

- Light tents are white fabric or nylon tents with an opening in front where you place your item. You then take the photo through the front part of the opening.

- Stands with solid-colored backgrounds can aid in cropping your photo.

- Reflectors are special umbrellas that spread out the light from your flash evenly.

Photo Tips

- Straight-on shot. Every item you sell should have at least one straight-on shot. This will most likely be the first shot that you are going to want them to see when they click on your item, so make sure you use this for your "free" first photo.

- Always use a contrasting background for your item. If your item is light, then use a dark background. If it is dark, use a light background. Just use those pieces of light and dark fabric that were mentioned earlier. Have one for the flat surface it is resting on and one for the backdrop.

- Do not try to take your pictures without having your camera rest on something stationary, like a tripod or a stool, at the same height as your item.

- Place your item on the floor and take your picture with your camera directly above it if you are trying to avoid light coming in from your windows.

- If you keep getting a bright spot on your item because of your flash, try either turning off your flash or using a diffuser to spread your light out more evenly.

- Get a few different angles and/or close-ups of your items. You can use these pictures in the description of your item so that customers can easily see any flaws or defects that the item you are selling may have.

- Do not get too close to your item with your camera. You do not want your item to be out of focus. Instead, use your zoom, or crop it later with your editing software to make it appear larger.

- If you want to show how big something is, reference it with something that the viewer will be able to compare. Some reference items that work well include a yard stick, a ruler, a quarter, or a pen. You can use any common, standard-sized item.

The Three Most Common Photographic Blunders

The following list contains the three most common blunders in eBay photography. The professional businessperson will learn to avoid these common mistakes.

1. **Beware of Glare**. Items that are prepackaged in cellophane will inevitably reflect light and produce an unsightly glare. The only solution to this problem is to take the item out of the wrapping to take the picture. If that is not an option, try taking the shot at an angle so that most of the reflected light will be deflected away from the camera, or you can experiment with using diffusers.

2. **Distracting Background**. If your background is too busy with scenery and other distractions, your product will not be given the emphasis it needs. Do not worry too much about creative backgrounds. Although they may make for good-looking pictures, you are going to want to stick to the trusted white or dark fabric backgrounds.

3. **Too Much Space**. Make your item the largest thing in the picture. Crop until you fill up most of the picture with your item. Do not make the customer squint to find your item, and do not let it be swallowed up by a gigantic field of your background. Instead, make sure you are doing your best to keep the item you are selling featured prominently in your photographs.

The eBay Cost

While it is nice to have pictures on your listing, in some cases, they are an investment, as eBay charges after the first picture. You can find the current list of fees at **http://pages.eBay.com/help/sell/fees.html**. There are different packages available to place more pictures on your auctions. Be mindful of these fees, as this is an area you can save on. You also want to figure in the price of the add-ons when figuring what price to list your item at.

The Process of Getting Pictures Ready

Your time is worth something, and if you are spending hours on what a picture looks like for a particular sale, you are more than likely taking time away from things that are important. Most of the time, your editing software can fix problems that will make your photos ready for publishing. Here are some tips that can help you create pictures fast and have them look good on your eBay listings.

- Make sure that the resolution of your image is set at 72 pixels per inch. It may not be the clearest resolution, but it will load faster on eBay.

- Do not set your camera any higher than 800x 600 when capturing images. It is optimized for posting while allowing you to have the option of cropping if you like. It will take up less memory and, therefore, will allow you to post more pictures.

- Try to keep your images to 480 pixels wide. This will give your image the size needed for clarity.

- Crop your photo as needed, and get rid of any unnecessary background.

- Change the contrast to make your image look its best.

- Always save your image as a .jpg file. This format works best on eBay.

- Try to keep the memory size of your image to 40 KB or less.

- Keep in mind that computer monitors usually are able to have a resolution of 72 pixels per inch.

- When you are scanning an image, they are measured at dots per inch, not pixels per inch. Scanned images are displayed at about 72 dots per inch. Do not confuse dots with pixels.

- Making your images look good on your monitor will make them look better online. If you compress an image, you will lose the sharpness of the image.

- Make sure you know where to find your images for easy upload. You should create an easily accessible file that just has images. When saving your images, give them names or dates that are recognizable. If you do not save them in any logical order, you will waste time flipping through images to upload.

CHAPTER 13

Finding the Best Products for the Cheapest Prices

There are thousands of places, online and otherwise, where you can buy nice wholesale goods. The problem is that everybody else on eBay has already bought goods from those places, and you will have nothing with which to differentiate yourself. eBay does not work well for people who sell commodity items. You need to find something more unusual that nobody else has.

As a PowerSeller, you must recognize that your eBay business is not about selling things on eBay. Selling is just a small part of it; the fun really begins before you have created the listing, when you are out trying to find the products to list. Sourcing your goods is what will make or break you. A bad product, no matter how well designed and well worded in your listing, is not going to make you any money. Your product mix, the quality, and the scarcity of what you acquire are going to determine your sell-through level.

What sets PowerSellers apart from amateur sellers is that they have already learned that they will not sell everything they list. There is a level of acceptable loss, and you will have to determine that on your own. You will have to figure in your acquisition costs, your eBay expenses, and your time involved. You will also have to determine what percentage of products you will have to sell to turn a profit. You may, for example, be acquiring goods at such a low cost that you are able to turn a good profit if you are only selling half of what you are listing.

PowerSelling Tip

Look for companies that are going out of business and have a large inventory they are trying to liquidate.

Mix it Up

In addition to where to find the products, you must also consider what products you want to find. If you can specialize in a few areas, you are more likely to become successful because you will become knowledgeable about those areas and get to know the collectors.

Nevertheless, you must also be cautious and avoid stagnation. eBay is a highly fluid market, and what sells well one month may not sell well the next. Do not get too attached to any one category, and do not be afraid to branch out. Think beyond the ordinary. There is money to be made in selling day-to-day products, but it is a little different on eBay than it is anywhere else. If you do insist on trading in ordinary commodity goods, you have to realize that you are selling something that eBay shoppers can probably get at a store within a few miles of their home, and you have to give them some incentive to buy it from you instead.

The incentive is usually price. Take those portable fluorescent light bulbs that people have started using to replace their regular bulbs. They are energy efficient, but you can also get them at any corner drugstore, usually for about $2 each. If you can somehow lay your hands on a shipment of them that has been deeply discounted, and you can sell them for $1 apiece, you will make money. However, if you list them on eBay for the same price they can get them at their neighborhood store, you are out of luck. You also have to figure in shipping costs. People will be more willing to pay for shipping if it is for an item that they cannot find anywhere else.

Put Items Together

You can make your products seem like a better deal sometimes if you package products together that complement one another. The idea here is to take two or more products, and instead of selling them in separate auctions, sell them as a set. You will increase your odds of selling both products in one sale, as opposed to selling only one.

Retailers do this all the time. Look at computer advertisements. When you buy a computer, many times, you do not just buy the computer. They sell a bundle that includes the computer, an inkjet printer, some software, and other assorted, odd peripherals. The result is that you get more money from each customer, you have better odds of selling all the products, and you save on your eBay listing fees.

Consumable Goods

Goods that get used up and have to be purchased again periodically are also a good sort of item to sell. If you are offering a good deal, you can get repeat business using this approach. Take something like inkjet cartridges. This market is highly competitive, and buyers are always looking for a deal. Granted, it is a commodity item, and they can be found anywhere. From that perspective, it is a hard sell on eBay, but if you can make a good pitch and offer them at a competitive price, you can make a sale.

Here is a secret that PowerSellers know. When you make a sale, you may not make that much profit on that one sale, but you get a customer that is likely to return several times to your shop to buy more. They are buying your company's reputation. If you can sell them something simple, in a way that meets their standards, a customer is more likely to buy from your company again.

If you are dealing in this type of consumable, make sure to build a mailing list so you can send out occasional reminders to your customers, so they will remember to come back to you when they need more. Offer special incentives to keep them coming back.

Tips from the Experts

Endicia is the coolest and best way to save money and time. Also, if I'm shipping Priority Mail, I make sure I use USPS Priority Mail boxes. I also save boxes from my incoming stock if they are clean and in good shape. My husband brings peanuts, bubble wrap, and air pockets home from work for my packing. I use a lot of bubble envelopes, and prices are constantly changing on them, so I always shop my four favorite eBay sellers for the best deal before buying.

Vendio for auction management is another way I run my business efficiently. I couldn't keep track of the number of items I carry in all the different permutations without a management and inventory service like Vendio. I especially like it because it is web-based, which means I can access all the information about auctions, payments, inventory, etc. from a computer.

— Charlene Anderson

In Your Own Backyard

Before you start looking for potential resources all over the world to find merchandise to sell, you should begin by searching all around you. There are many different places you can go to find all sorts of stuff to turn a profit with on eBay. Around your hometown are resources that you may not realize exist. The advantage of local sourcing, too, is that you will save on shipping costs. eBay sellers who deal in collectibles, antiques, arts, and crafts are especially adept at finding things locally. Of course, you do not want to pay their retail price, but remember, these people do not have a huge market and are always looking for a sale. Tell them about your eBay business, and ask for a volume discount. It may well be that they have thought of selling on eBay but have not gotten around to it, do not have the time or inclination, or do not have a computer.

When you engage in local buying, you are bound to get people who hear about it and will constantly come around and offer you things. While sometimes, you can actually get good deals this way, more often than not, these people have an inflated sense of what their item is really worth, so you will have to do some serious bargaining with them. On the other hand, they may just be looking for a few extra dollars, and you can get some good deals if you know what to look for and can separate the trash from the treasure.

There are eBay sellers who will go where no others like to go to find their treasures. They root through dumpsters and pull out discarded odds and ends. They then take them to an acquaintance of theirs who deals on eBay and attempt to sell these discards. Surprisingly, they are often successful. Of course, not everyone wants to drive through alleys picking through people's trash cans, but the point is that you can find saleable items almost anywhere.

Online Bulletin Boards

An online bulletin board is a locally or nationally recognized site where people post all types of information, such as apartments for rent, services being offered, jobs available in the area, and things that people are trying to sell. More often than not, there is some nominal fee charged for people to post something for a certain amount of time. You will be surprised at some of the deals you will come across if you keep an eye out for some items that people in and around your own neighborhood post on such sites. Two of the most nationally-used online bulletin boards are **Craigslist.org** and **Sellstufflocal.com**. Both allow you to look at listings according to geographic location.

Be on the lookout for Web boards that are set up specifically for certain areas. For instance, if you live in Florida, **Ocala4Sale.com** is an exceptional online bulletin board that you certainly do not want to ignore. Do some Internet research to see whether there are any popular Web boards in your area.

Local Storage Companies

Storage facilities are excellent places to pick up some items that you will easily be able to turn a profit with. Most people use storage facilities to store things that they do not want to part with, but that they have no room for in their home or apartment. They pay a fee for the storage facility to store it for them. Most of these places just offer you a small, garage-like area, or a room where you can go and store your items yourself. Occasionally, the owner of the items in storage stops paying rent, and after a period of trying to get in touch with the owner of the items, the storage facility is free to dispose of them any way they see fit.

This is where you come in. Contact all your local storage facilities and find out when they hold their regular auctions to get rid of unclaimed items to make room for new renters. Sometimes, you may have to buy an entire set without ever getting to see what is in there, but chances are, if they went through all the trouble in the first place to store it, there must be at least some items of value contained in there.

Even if most of the items in there have little or no resale value, you are likely going to find some gems that will make the whole purchase worth it. Donate the rest of the stuff that you are not going to be able to turn a profit on to a local charity, and get a receipt for a tax write-off.

Flea Markets

Selling at a flea market can be a frustrating experience. If the weather is too good, people frequently have better things to do than browse a flea market, and if the weather is bad, then people do not want to be walking around. The most frustrating things for vendors at flea markets is that regardless of the quality of the merchandise they are selling, most people think of flea markets as giant yard sales. They are going there looking for a bargain, and they will not want to pay top dollar for your items.

For you as a reseller, flea markets can be a gold mine. Find out when there are going to be flea markets in your area, and plan on going. If the weather is too good or too lousy, count your blessings and go anyway. Dress comfortably, and try to find those vendors who are so desperate to part with some of their goods that they are willing to bring down their prices to make a sale. You will be surprised at what people will overlook at a flea market that you can buy and resell for a large profit.

Try to make many contacts as well. Most veterans of flea markets are hoarders of treasures and junk. Most likely, what they have brought that day represents only a small portion of what they have at their homes. If you are looking for some particular products, mention them in passing as you are going about your day. You never know when someone may say, "Oh yeah, I have a box of that in my basement." Many resalable items can be obtained in this way.

Yard Sales

Yard sales come in all shapes and sizes. You will have all different types of sellers at yard sales: people who are looking to get rid of what they consider crap, people who are looking to raise money, and people who have other motivations for putting some tables up and selling all sorts of things at cheap prices.

Your basic strategy for going to yard sales should be to identify all the ones that are happening in your area by checking out local listings on a weekly basis, and then plan to go as early as possible so that you can snatch up any gems that may be there. Then, go back late, just as they are cleaning up, and see what you can snatch up. Offer to buy all of something or everything they have left for a price that will not offend them, but one that you are sure to be able to turn a profit on. For instance, let's say that you bought a vintage record player at 6 a.m. for $10 that you know you are going to get at least $100 for. You noticed that in the corner there were a couple of boxes of books. Books will regularly sell on eBay, and these are priced at $1 per book. You estimate that there are about 100 titles. When you come back later, as they are beginning to pack up for the day, you notice that not many of the books have sold. You offer to take all of the books off their hands for about $25. They agree, eager to be rid of them. You later go on to sell each book for about $5 to $10 dollars, making a respectable profit.

Go to your local yard sales, snatch up the obvious moneymakers early, and then take notes about which sales you are going to come back to later when they are closing, because there are many items you may be able to buy all together for one low price.

PowerSelling Tip

If possible, have someone you know available to do a quick Internet search for items while you are out rummaging or auctioning. You may have a hunch about an item, and finding out whether an item sells well on eBay is a smart move before buying.

Church Bazaars

Church bazaars are excellent places to get potential merchandise. Frequently, they have higher quality products than those available at flea markets and garage sales. Church members may be trying to raise money for a specific cause, so they are not likely to bring out stuff that they just want to get rid of.

It may still be worthwhile to show up early so that you can see whether they are selling any valuable antiques or under-priced gems, but what you are in actuality looking for is items that you are going to come back for later. Arrive as they are packing away crates and offer to take a box of something off their hands. You might easily pick up that box of several hundred DVDs that they were going to sell for $1 apiece for $20 to $40. After a day of serving the needs of their church, volunteers will be eager to be rid of as much as possible, rather than having to put everything away.

Newspapers

Your local newspapers can be a quality source of potential goods. Get into the habit of checking local newspaper classified listings every day as you sip your morning coffee. Many times, people will announce all sorts of things like flea markets, yard sales, and church bazaars, but they will also post items that they are trying to sell. You may see furniture that you can resell, cars that can be auctioned on eBay autos, or even houses and other forms of real estate that you can buy and resell for a nice profit.

Also, be on the lookout for "collections" that an heir or a divorced spouse may not appreciate, books, costume jewelry, computer parts, games, electronics, art, comic books, videos, coins, stamps, old photos, rare baseball cards, or anything else that has been inherited or is no longer wanted.

Auctions

Auctions can be excruciating to sit through, with the monotone voice of the auctioneer droning on, but they can be a significant source of products to sell. Do some research and find out what kinds of auctions are going on in your area. Distributors often hold public auctions to get rid of merchandise that has not sold. If you go to a live auction, stay to the absolute end. They frequently bring out the good stuff near the end. You may have to go through hour after hour of useless merchandise before one or two gems come onto the stage. Drink plenty of coffee. Even if you are just barely keeping your eyes open, stick with it. Think of it as a part of your job. You will likely be grateful that you did.

Thrift Stores

There are many charity-run thrift stores that are nationally distributed. Goodwill, the Salvation Army, and other local charities often resell donated items to help raise money for their organizations. You will meet many people there looking for things to resell, just like you, and the community that can develop at these thrift stores can be a valuable source of insight and encouragement for your own business.

Big corporations know the value of hiring consultants, whose value to the company is the knowledge and experience they bring to the table. They often pay their consultants large fees to attend meetings. Since you are likely not a multi-billion dollar company and cannot offer large monetary incentives, you must find other ways to gain friends who have been doing this much longer than you. These are the "old-timers" who can look at a pile of "junk" and immediately see the treasure scattered here and there. These are the people you want to get to know.

You will almost easily be able to differentiate the professional like yourself from the run-of-the-mill junk collector. Offer to help them sift through the thrift store's collections in exchange for some free advice and friendship.

You might even want to look into getting to know the owners of the thrift stores. Offering them the opportunity to become a trade assistant is an excellent way to have them put high quality items to the side for you to look at first, in exchange for you sharing some of your profits with them. They likely would rather help you and get part of the profits then let something that they know the intrinsic value of sit on a shelf and collect dust.

As a seller who has established yourself as someone who can effectively market and sell things in the online world, you have a valuable skill that you can share with others to make not only yourself money, but others as well.

Again, large companies understand the value of this profit sharing. They have no problem letting different companies share in some of their profits if they can be sure that the business venture is going to make more money for everyone than any single company could make on its own; learn from them. Especially if you can find a thrift store run by knowledgeable people, it pays to share a small percentage of your profits in exchange for friends who are going to call you first when that valuable crate of stuff gets dropped off at their front door.

Estate Auctions

Sometimes, when a person dies or a bank has seized the entire estate of an individual, there will be auctions where almost an entire lifetime of collected stuff will go on sale to the highest bidders. Check your local listings and Web boards; you will be surprised how many estate auctions go on in your area on a regular basis. Attending one a week can be a valuable source of items and income. You never know what types of treasures were left behind. Often, grieving relatives, who always will have first pick, will take items of sentimental, rather than monetary, value.

Attend all the estate auctions you can, and once again, make sure you stay until the absolute end. Keep your eye out for collections that you can easily sell to make a nice profit. Even if you do not have dreams of quitting your day job and doing eBay full-time, attending one estate auction a week can turn into a fun hobby, and an incredibly satisfying second income.

When attending these estate auctions, it is absolutely vital to do a complete walkthrough several times over. Have an idea of what you are willing to spend beforehand. Be willing to bid on the contents of an entire table, even though most of the items may be going to charity for a tax write-off; bid on tables where there are the items of significant resale value to make the whole purchase worth it. If you live close enough to the auction location, go home and check out the value of some questionable items that caught your eye. A laptop with an Internet card that can pick up a broadband signal like a cell phone is an exceptional resource to have on these little excursions. It will make your life much easier by allowing you to look up things right away without having to leave.

Occasionally, you will have the opportunity to bid on the contents of an entire estate. If you can afford it, do it. Especially if you have done a walk-through and seen many items that can be resold, you will have significantly increased your amount of product, and will also have plenty of stuff to donate to lower your tax bracket.

eBay Reseller Market

As a PowerSeller, you will have the ability to use the site **http://reseller.eBay.com/ns/home.html**. This site allows you to buy directly from wholesalers and manufacturers. You will be able to access excess inventory, buy in lots in quantities suitable for resale by small and medium-sized businesses, and you can but the inventory immediately, with no long-term or minimum-volume commitments.

Moving Beyond the Neighborhood

After establishing yourself in the local neighborhood, you may want to start branching out into the wider world. As your business grows, your potential source of inventory must grow with it. This is especially true if you start getting some regular traffic on specific types of goods; you are going to want to start thinking more in terms of the bigger picture.

All the ways we discussed of finding products in your own area are excellent ways to get large quantities of things to sell. Yet, one thing that they will not be a good source of is the same types of products on a continual basis. The best types of things to sell are the type of products that you have an interest in and of which you have a working knowledge. That does not mean that you cannot make a profit off digital cameras when you do not have an interest in digital photography, but if you want staying power in this industry, you are going to want to deal with products in which you have some degree of specialty.

That is where the wider world comes in. You will find plenty of reliable sources of high-quality goods with excellent prices if you just take the time to find them. This section will give you the inside track to some of the secrets of finding sources for the best products that are out there, just waiting.

After building small and establishing a product for the market, and building up positive feedback from established customers, start thinking bigger; look into the following potential product sources. When thinking about buying large lots, ask for samples or buy a couple first to sell on eBay to see their potential to generate sales.

Trade Shows

Trade shows are where suppliers, wholesalers, and manufacturers exhibit their products throughout the country and the world. The benefits of attending trade shows are many. Not only will you be able to network and gain key contacts from all over the country, you will also get to see and try out new products, all under the same roof.

Do not forget to register yourself as a legitimate business; your tax ID number will open the door for you to get into many trade shows that are closed to the public. A tax ID number is not hard to get from your local authorities, and if you do not have one already, you should get one as soon as possible. It gives you an edge over all those on eBay who have not gone through the trouble to register themselves as a business.

Do your research right and go to the trade shows that are going to be featuring a category of merchandise that you specialize in. You will get to see the latest up-and-coming trends in your niche market. Even if all you were able to afford was to go to one of these shows a year, it would help you stay current on all the latest trends.

Find the next trade show you can attend at **www.biztradeshows.com**.

PowerSelling Tip

Look for the Better Business Bureau's (BBB) Online Reliability logo on Web sites of wholesalers, distributors, and drop-shippers. Clicking on the BBB's logo on these sites should take you to the Better Business Bureau's Web site, where you will see a message stating the company's compliance. If the logo does not take you to the BBB's site, or it takes you to a site that does not begin with **www.bbb.org***, then report it immediately to the Better Business Bureau.*

Direct Manufacturers

Frequently, direct manufacturers work with only large-scale wholesalers who can buy large quantities of their products at a reduced rate. Most of the time, they will not deal directly with someone like you, who will not buy anywhere near the amount of bulk items a large-sale wholesaler would. Nevertheless, many of the smaller manufacturers who are based in your area may be willing to deal directly with you. Be polite and professional with them; if you assure them that they will be getting continued business with your company, you stand a good chance of them wanting your business. At worst, you will get a list of wholesalers, and at best, you will cut out the middleman and deal directly with the manufacturer.

If you find a company that makes what you want to sell, contact them and try to get a list of wholesalers who carry their products. Although you will not get as good a rate as the wholesalers are getting, you still should be able to get a quality deal on bulk orders.

Also, there are custom manufacturers who will regularly deal in almost any-sized order. They make custom products, like pens with your company name on them, graphic tees with whatever you want on them, mugs, banners, and other such customizable items. You can run a t-shirt company online by having a custom manufacturer make them for you. For instance, you can have them make a bunch of t-shirts for you that say, "I bought this shirt on eBay!" and sell them out of your eBay store. They will make them for you in a variety of sizes and colors. All you have to do is sell them and ship them.

Do your homework. Most manufacturers will have no problem selling you a bunch of products they know no one is buying. In the end, they will be out to make a sale. Do some research on the marketability of the items you are looking to purchase.

Remanufacturers

Remanufactured products are not new, and they are not exactly used either. They are products that have been returned to the manufacturer for one reason or another, repaired, cleaned, and put back into new packaging. Many consumers love them because they are getting a product that in most cases is like new, but at a better price. Many remanufactured goods even have some existing warranties attached to them.

Since most major retailers do not like dealing with remanufactured goods (although Macintosh has caught on to this consumer trend and sells remanufactured items right from their retailers), you have an excellent advantage if you can buy these remanufactured goods from the manufacturers; this is especially true with electronics. Most manufacturers will jump at the chance to get the merchandise off their hands; they will be willing to sell it to you for a reduced price, which you can mark up, and it will still end up costing the consumer much less than buying the same product new.

Make sure you do your homework and check with the manufacturers who deal in products that you like to sell to see whether they have any remanufactured merchandise they would like to part with.

PowerSelling Tip

Deal with manufacturers directly. Do not use intermediaries, as you can get better deals dealing with directly with the manufacturer.

Distributors

There are thousands of distributors out there who offer large catalogs full of wholesale-priced goods to people like flea marketers, craft show folk, and, of course, eBay sellers. You can find many of these places on the Internet. Some of these distributors are merely companies that re-distribute items from other distributors, and you must proceed with caution.

Beware of advertisements that claim that you can re-sell their product at an exceptionally high profit. If they are selling an item to you for $5 a dozen, and their ad says "retail price $19.99 each!" then you may do best to move on to the next place. There are unrealistic claims out there.

Another thing to look out for when dealing with these sorts of wholesale distributors, especially if they are not local, is that the picture on the Web site may look much better than the actual product. If you are interested in a particular item, find out whether you can buy just one as a sample to inspect before placing a larger order. If they are not willing to sell you a single piece, that is a big red flag.

Finally, while you may be able to find some good products at attractive wholesale prices from these distributors, there are thousands of others who are doing the same thing. These are stock items, and if you try to re-sell them on eBay, you may be surprised to find that there are 100 other people selling exactly the same thing.

Drop-Shippers

Like the wholesale distributors, drop-shippers also offer goods to thousands of resellers, many of which deal on eBay. The advantage of a drop-shipper, though, is that you do not have to buy large quantities of any one product, and you do not have to worry about shipping. The drop-shipper ships out the product on your behalf, using an address label that reflects the name of your own eBay shop.

Naturally, there are some inherent limitations with this approach. Countless others may be offering the same thing. Drop-shippers make their money by getting small merchants to offer their catalog under their own name.

But if you do not want to package, ship, and keep track of multiple items, then drop-shipping is the only way to go. One of the most comprehensive lists of drop-shippers is the Drop-ship Source Directory. You can easily eliminate middlemen simply by using this directory, which is by far the most up-to-date list you will find, and it is quite useful for all your Internet businesses.

While drop-shipping is a legitimate business and can be quiet profitable, there are many drop-shipping scams out there. A purported drop-shipper may merely be an intermediary who claims he is the actual supplier. Also, the goods you are representing may be substandard. You lose an element of quality control when using a drop-shipper, since you are not personally inspecting the items. It is easy to make a poor quality product look good in a picture. However, when customers get the product, and it is not what they expected, they will not blame the invisible drop-shipper; they will blame you. Avoid drop-shipping frauds and establish an online business or eBay presence by using only reputable, reliable drop-shippers.

A variation of this process is a fulfillment service, which does not supply the products, but takes your products, which you have personally selected, stores them, and completes the fulfillment process on your behalf. Numerous reputable suppliers are more than willing to do drop-shipping or fulfillment on your behalf. They may require an account set-up fee that you will need to pay, so you will need to be prepared for some initial investment, but always carefully investigate all related costs before agreeing to anything in writing.

A simple online search is a good way to find suppliers who do drop-shipping, but many companies are more interested in taking money from you than in helping you make money. This is a shortsighted approach on their part, because when you make money, they do too. However, as in all occupations, many do not understand this simple principle. Find a drop-shipper who is reputable, willing to talk to you in person, and who will send you actual physical samples of products for your review before you buy in bulk.

Some issues to clarify before starting a business relationship with any drop-shipper are:

- How much will they charge you for the merchandise, including any handling charges they might pass on to you for storing, packaging, and shipping the item?

- Precisely how will the charges be processed? Are you required to pay as you go, as they ship each item, or will they send you an invoice monthly?

- Do they accept returns directly from your buyers in the event that the merchandise should be damaged?

The advantage of using a drop-shipper is that you do not need to have an on-site inventory, have a need to package and ship anything or have to have a place to store your merchandise. It is a great way to do business, but you must be careful who you do business with and what agreements that are made, because it could cost you a lot of money if you are careless. Here are some tips when considering a particular drop-shipper. These are questions you should be asking before you sign any agreement with a drop-ship company.

- Make sure that there is no minimum purchase that you must sell of the drop-shippers products.
- Do have to agree to sell only their items on your web store or on eBay, or can you sell other products?
- Will you have the ability to pick the items you wish to sell from their inventory or will you be required to sell items that they chose.
- Does the drop-shipper provide descriptions and pictures of their products to post on eBay or your web store?
- What is the process of getting an item shipped? Do they require payment from you first, or will they bill you for the product monthly?
- Do their product prices include shipping or is this separate? Who do they use to ship and where are they willing to ship to?
- How quickly will the item be sent out to the drop-shipper? Do they have a guarantee?

Here is the general way that a drop-shipper works.

- You chose the items you wish to sell on eBay and in your store.
- You post the items and place them on eBay for bidding.
- A buyer finds the item and buys it.
- You send the drop-shipper a payment, usually by credit card.

- The drop-shipper gets the order and sends it out immediately.
- You keep the difference between what the item cost you buying it from the drop-shipper and the price the buyer paid.

Many other PowerSellers use drop-shipping companies as the source of the products that they sell. Everyone gets the same picture and description of the product. In order to catch the eye of a buyer you may consider posting your own pictures and descriptions that you create. You need to do whatever it takes to set your business aside from every other eBay store. This takes a little extra work, but this will translate into higher profits later on.

Do not be dragged into the trap of trying to sell the thousands of items that the drop-shipper has to offer. You will be killed in fees and your sales will be low. Stick with a niche market. Specialize in certain types of products. Know everything about those products and be able to talk like an expert about those products. Blog about the products you have to sell and get the word out.

Another trap to avoid is those drop-shippers that make you pay a fee just to view their catalog. You should not have to pay anything to see the products that they want you to sell for them. You should also consider buying a few of the items you are considering selling. Try them out for yourself. You do not want to sell junk, because there is plenty of that on eBay as it is. You want to sell high end quality products for a competitive price.

Look for drop-shippers that are offering a healthy number of products and ones that fall into the niche that you wish to sell. Avoid those that boost that they can ship thousands of different kinds of products. Some of these companies are merely a middle man and are buying from wholesalers. This can cause a delay in filling your orders and they may not be able to offer you the best prices available.

Do not be fooled by claims that their products have a high resale value. Do your research and look at how much their products are selling for on eBay compared to what they are saying that their products will sell for. Do not be taken in by inflated claims. Trust worthy companies will not need to inflate their claims; their history and low prices will speak for themselves. You may even find that some reputable wholesalers will also function as a drop-shipper for your company.

If you sell your item, go to the distributor's site, and find it is not in stock, call the drop-shipper. It is possible that they still have the item in the warehouse and simply took it off the Web site because it was running low.

If that is not the case, you will have to contact your buyers and admit that the items they bought are currently not on hand with your supplier. It is imperative that you call your customers in this situation; they may not be as angry as they might be if you had just e-mailed this information. It would be wise to offer to refund their money in full immediately, possibly even send some kind of consolation offering. Someone else's error may net you negative feedback. That risk is inherent in employing drop-shipping as a routine business practice.

Online Wholesalers

You can find anything online these days, but be careful, as anyone can publish a Web site that says they are an Internet wholesaler and may just be out to get as many credit card numbers as possible. Do not buy from an online wholesaler who will not give you a physical address and phone number. However, look around online, as many legitimate vendors can get you wholesale products.

One of the most popular Internet wholesalers out there is Liquidation.com. Check them out, and be aware that there are many other eBay wholesalers who would be a wonderful resource for products to drive your sales into the PowerSeller status. You should also check out **www.wholesale-central.com** and **www.biglotswholesale.com**. While **www.greatrep.com** sells wholesale giftware and home furnishings, www.bargainw.com deals in wholesale dollar merchandise. They have plenty of consumables, health and beauty aids, stationery items, kitchen supplies, candy, toys, cleaning supplies, plastic lines, and house wares.

Tips from the Experts

Here are some tips that can be useful for up-and-coming PowerSellers.

- *Always be growing your e-mail mailing list.*
- *Diversify your online presence to include other non-eBay activities.*
- *Create information products as a great source of high-margin income.*
- *Always be automating, outsourcing, and setting up new income streams.*
- *Don't get tied to one product line too long. Competition will beat you eventually.*
- *Tell the world that you are an eMarketing consultant. Many people are fascinated by eBay and Internet marketing, and you know more than they do. This is a great source of potential income.*
- *Stay creative.*

— Jim Cockrum

PowerSelling Tip

Terms that might be helpful to know when dealing in the wholesale industry:

- *Jobber: Someone who buys merchandise to sell at liquidated prices or salvages merchandise.*
- *Job Lot: This is the term to refer to selling a lot of merchandise at one time. The items in a job lot are often mismatched sizes, unusual colors, and some may just be junk. Be aware that some of it can be damaged.*
- *Off-Price Lots: These are usually end-of-season overruns that are sold by manufacturers. Much of this merchandise ends up in outlet stores.*
- *Liquidations: These are some of the best deals, but the amount you have to buy at one time may be large, which can lead to problems, such as cost and storage. You must be aware that much of what comes in a liquidation lot may not be useable or saleable.*

Using eBay as a Source

The range of the "type" of sellers on eBay is wide and highly diverse. You have your professional PowerSellers, the intermediates who are just taking off, hobbyists, scam artists, and the seller who occasionally has some items to sell.

Because eBay is so huge, at any given moment, there can be hundreds of casual sellers who are trying to make a profit. Normally, these people have stuff that they simply do not want anymore, and, instead of throwing it away or packing it in a basement, they have decided to sell it on eBay. Often, they do this to help pay for the new thing that they now want.

More often than not, since they have already gotten some use and enjoyment out of the product, and they did not buy it specifically to get any resale profit, they will sell their items below the lowest selling price of similarly listed products on eBay. This way, they can guarantee that their products will be the first to go.

This is a potential gold mine if you deal in items of a certain type, such as DVDs, CDs, books, or video and computer games. There are many people selling things on eBay who are not trying to make a return on their investment, but are just trying to get whatever they can for stuff they no longer want. Therefore, they regularly post their products for the lowest possible price, since they did not supply an original overhead. Get in the habit of checking eBay's listings to learn to spot the casual buyer who is selling products below normal prices.

PowerSelling Tip

Check with any artists or crafters to be sure that they are not making their products from plans or patterns that are copyrighted or copying a registered or trademarked product from another company. All artistic and handmade items should be made using the crafter's original ideas and designs.

Trading Assistants

Seriously consider the value of becoming a trading assistant. A trading assistant is a person who will bring a seller items that they want them to sell for them. In exchange, the seller will receive a commission on the sale; this is a form of profit sharing. You could make a respectable income on just profit sharing alone, as long as you have a steady flow of inventory from contacts that are consistently looking for something to sell.

One of the pros to this type of business model is that there is no inventory that you need to go obtain. The inventory is literally brought to you. Also, you are not technically buying the inventory to resell. This can also be an excellent way for a beginner to get started in their eBay business, because then, you can do it without any start-up cost.

Start small, with your own neighborhood; find out whether you know of anyone, or whether anyone knows of someone, who is looking to get rid of stuff and would be willing to share the profits for someone doing all the work for them. Check out all the local resources for goods that we talked about earlier; get to know the owners of the thrift stores and the runners of the church bazaars, and check with your local manufactures to see whether they want help unloading some unwanted goods.

You can be the person everyone comes to sell their unwanted items, and the business can be run with the model that no one pays any money up front. Using this model, everyone makes some money. They should make the larger share of the profit, and you should decide what an acceptable amount of profit is for you. Make sure you factor in the price of the listing fees and the other costs that are going to be associated with adequately marketing the products for them.

Also, even if this is not the primary way that you make your eBay income, this type of model can be seamlessly integrated into any business plan. Diversification is the key. Make sure you are getting potential products from all sorts of sources. Being a trading assistant is a way of making sure you have staying power in your industry.

There are similar requirements to those that you must achieve in order to maintain a PowerSeller status.

- You must sell at least ten items per month in the past three months.
- You must maintain a rating of 100 or higher, and you must have 98 percent positive feedback.

Obtaining Merchandise Checklist

- I have made a list of subjects that I am proficient in or have special knowledge about to consider as possible product lines.

- I have done some research to determine whether the things I know about are being bought regularly on eBay and, if so, how many people are selling these items.

- I have evaluated how much space I have at my disposal for storage of inventory to help me decide whether I can work with wholesalers who sell in bulk or whether I should consider a drop-shipping relationship with a supplier.

- I have made a list of local manufacturers or distributors who may be sources of merchandise.

- I have considered the pros and cons of purchasing used items locally and decided whether I will include these as a merchandise source.

- If I am planning to create custom products for sale, I am aware of all copyright laws and how they may apply to the items I am making.

CHAPTER 14

Work Smarter, Not Harder

PowerSelling Tip

You can learn even more about selling on eBay from experts like those mentioned in this book at eBay university, at ***http://pages.eBay.com/university****. They offer two levels of classes: Selling Basics and Beyond Selling Basics. The good thing is that the educators live in your neighborhood. You just have to plug in your city and it will give you a list of instructors.*

The Customer is First

Just because you have an Internet business does not mean everything has to be automated. Providing excellent, personalized customer service is essential and will help build a larger base of returning customers.

The greatest mistake made when starting an Internet business of any sort, including an eBay business, is to think that because it is online, you can remove yourself from the equation and become anonymous. Too many people want to start an Internet business, but do not list their address, phone number, or contact information, saying, "I do not want to be bothered," or "I do not want a bunch of people calling me at all hours."

You are in business. Part of the deal is that you are going to be bothered, and people will call you at all hours. Accept it and get used to it. Nobody ever said becoming a PowerSeller was convenient or easy. If you go out of your way to become inaccessible, you will not get as much business. Yes, you will get the occasional midnight call, and once in a while, somebody who is just crazy. It is all part of the package. Being a PowerSeller is hard work, but if you are smart about it, you can reduce your work by becoming efficient and organized.

PowerSelling Tip

Consider forming alliances with other companies. This will help you grow and share some costs.

When Are You Open?

Part of the attraction of becoming a seller on eBay is that you get to choose your own hours, for the most part. You may have found out that it is not as easy as you thought, and ultimately, you will work harder being self-employed than you ever did as an employee. While it is true that you will have more flexibility, you will still have deadlines to meet, packages to get out on time to meet commitments to customers, and, more than likely, you will find yourself creating a schedule for yourself. You do not have to overwork yourself; you just have to come up with a workable schedule.

If you are not a "morning" person, you can goof off until noon and then work until 8 p.m. if you want, as long as you meet your commitments and make yourself available. Many PowerSellers find themselves taking calls and sending out e-mails at all hours of the day, from early morning until late at night. Suppose you live in Bangkok, which is 12 hours ahead of Eastern Standard Time; you may take calls at 3 a.m. to accommodate customers in the United States.

Regardless of how you arrange your workday, it is best from an organizational point of view if you apply some measure of regularity to it, and most importantly, meet your deadlines. You may decide that you prefer to work only on Tuesdays, Wednesdays, and Thursdays, and if your business is not that big, that may be adequate. However, if you want to be a PowerSeller, you will have to have a greater commitment than that. Even if you decide to work those days, on your days off, there will still be e-mails coming in. Orders will be arriving in your e-mail box. People may be calling you, wondering whether you could find a particular item for them, and these people must be accommodated. That is why even on your days off, you will do well to spend an hour answering your e-mails and taking care of things that need an immediate response.

PowerSelling Tip

Look for items that are inexpensive to process and ship but can be sold for high prices. These will make you the maximum profit.

What Buyers Expect of PowerSellers

Among all businesses, online or otherwise, eBay has perhaps the highest expectations of good service than any other. Buyers know that they can demand it and expect it. They know that if an eBay seller provides poor service, they will get a negative feedback, and after a few negative feedbacks, that seller will be out of business.

The feedback system is a bit unforgiving, but it is the way eBay operates. Every business, at one time or another, has probably had a dissatisfied customer, but eBay is the only one that allows those dissatisfied customers to post their complaints where all the other customers can see. When you go to the grocery store, and the bagger puts your bread on the bottom of the bag and crushes it, the manager may give you another loaf of bread, but he certainly would not let you write in marker on the front window, "My bread was crushed here. Avoid checkout lane six." eBay is the only business I know of that allows this sort of public feedback.

This system likely exists because it is not eBay that will be put out of business by bad feedback, it is the eBay seller. There are millions of sellers. One less will not make any difference. It is precisely this brutal feedback system that has raised customer expectations. With eBay, the customer has tremendous power, far more power than with any other sales venue. As PowerSeller, you have to work within this framework, and customer service has to be a high priority for you.

Recently, eBay changed its policy about leaving negative feedback about buyers. You can leave comments, but you cannot leave a bad score. This even further unbalances the system in favor of the buyer. You must work hard to keep your rating high. It is your lifeblood.

PowerSelling Tip

Convince your suppliers that you have eBay skills that can benefit them.

Replying To E-Mail

If you have good items up for auction, chances are, you will get at least a few e-mails asking questions for nearly every item you have. First, try to respond to these e-mails as quickly as you can.

Never take more than 24 hours to respond. Ideally, you should check your e-mails and send out responses several times a day. Some sellers check many times an hour. This may seem like diligence, but this level of dedication can lead to burn out. You will find you are working all the time, and you will never be off the clock. Instead, schedule times you intend to check your e-mail.

Often, since auctions are listed with items with the ending time ending soonest, buyers may not even see your auction until the last day of the sale. On that last day, you will get the most action, and you are likely to get e-mail questions up until a few hours before the auction's closing. If you have auctions closing soon, check for e-mails frequently.

If you still have a day job, and cannot check your eBay business's e-mail during the day, make note of this in your "About Me" page and with your listing. A simple note to the effect of, "e-mails will be answered promptly between the hours of 5 p.m. and 10 p.m. daily" will suffice. As a Power-Seller, you will be working more than full-time, but it is still all right to have certain times in which you check e-mail and reply.

It does not have to take as long as you might think. Over time, you will see patterns in the e-mail queries, and you can develop "stock" answers. While you do not want to send a completely cut-and-paste form letter addressed "Dear Customer," you can have a set of cut-and-paste responses that you can use.

The trick here is to create e-mails and templates that you can use to create responses that are customized and personalized at the same time. Address the person by name every time. Paste in the appropriate "stock" response, but then take a moment to look it over to make sure it fits. You may need to tweak a word or a sentence here or there to make sure it is appropriate. In this way, you are able to send a response that is quick, personalized, and does not take much of your time.

Make sure that your e-mails are professional-sounding and well written. If you send an e-mail full of abbreviations, misspellings, and poor grammar, it will turn off your customers. They will think you are unprofessional and sloppy, and you will lose business. Write in a conversational, friendly style, but at the same time, make sure it is well written. Use your spell-checker. If you have a hard time composing a well-written sentence, do not do it yourself; hire somebody else to do it for you. Sending a poorly written e-mail is worse than sending no e-mail at all.

You will occasionally get an e-mail that sounds less than intelligent, but treat all customers with respect, even if the question they are asking is unusual or obviously unnecessary. Suppose you list a cashmere scarf. Your heading reads, "Brand New Cashmere Scarf from India." You get the following e-mail:

"HAY THERE GOOD AUCTION WHATS THAT SCARV MADE OF AND IS IT USED? WHERE IT COME FROM???"

You would be surprised at how many e-mails like this you will receive from people who just do not read your listing closely. Your first instinct is to ignore an e-mail like this, but ours is not to judge our customers. The fact that your customer did not read your listing correctly or write a coherent sentence does not mean that they are not going to buy what you have to offer. The fact that their questions could have been answered had they only read the heading of your listing is beside the point, and you do not need to point that out to them. Firing off an e-mail, "Read the listing. Your questions are answered there," may seem to make sense, but it is not going to make you any customers. Of course, they missed the information in the listing, did not read it, or just did not pay attention. Answer their e-mail promptly and politely, addressing each of their questions. Make no mention of the fact that they should have just read your auction heading. Sign off by saying, "If you have any other questions, please feel free to contact me again." This customer has money to spend, just like anybody else. Never make your customer feel unintelligent for asking the wrong question.

PowerSelling Tip

You can make a little extra money by offering companies a way to auction their items they might have thrown away.

When Do I Quit My Day Job?

Taking the plunge from simple seller to full-time PowerSeller can be a scary transition. The day job is a source of security, and most of us are tempted to hang onto it. If you have what is conventionally considered a "good job," then many well-meaning people, especially friends and family, are going to tell you, "You better hang onto that job."

What you must do is smile, nod, and ignore everything they say. You can provide yourself with just as much security as any employer can, no matter how large and apparently secure they may be. In fact, you can provide yourself with more, because you have direct control over your business.

When you think of your day job, you think of a company that gives you a paycheck regularly, and you tend to believe that your place of business will always be there. However, all things are impermanent. Corporate promises get broken, layoffs happen, and people get fired. Companies downsize or go out of business.

Quitting your day job, once you rid yourself of the illusion of job security, becomes a simple business decision. If you have reached the point in your eBay business when you are spending an inordinate amount of nights and weekends on it, you have perhaps hired a part-time assistant, your eBay income equals or exceeds the income from your day job, and you have plenty of money in the bank, it should be an easy decision to let go of the day job.

PowerSelling Tip

A good place to find answers to questions and to get to know other users is the community boards on eBay. There are different boards for different topics. You can access them at ***http://forums.eBay.com/category/eBay-Discussion-Boards/2001****.*

CHAPTER 15

Developing and Using a Business Plan

Tips from the Experts

The fear of leaving a "real" job to become your own boss is tough. There's a sense of security in having a regular paycheck. It's false security if you ask me, but still — it's hard to walk away from it.

It's also been hard "handing over" portions of my business to other people. It's so easy to fall into the habit of doing it all by yourself. It's easy to think that you are the best person to do it, but it can turn into a total waste of time and suck the energy and creativity right out of you if you aren't careful. The lesson I've learned is to hire competent help and always be outsourcing the "dirty work". Anything that is repetitive should be done by someone else. That was probably the biggest hurdle I faced. After I made the leap, though, the ideas have just been flowing, and I launch new income streams almost monthly now.

— Jim Cockrum

The difference between being a success or failure on eBay has to do with your mindset going into it. If you treat it like the business that it is, you will be fine. One secret that corporate Chief Executive Officers (CEO) know that many small business owners do not is the value of the business plan. Since this book is geared toward advanced sellers, I cannot stress the concept of having a functional business plan enough, as it can be one of the most powerful business tools. It is the blueprint upon which a successful small business is built. I encourage new business owners to develop a business plan early on, and as a PowerSeller, it is essential if you truly want to maximize your income and sales.

It takes more than just motivation and products to be a PowerSeller. It also takes research and planning. Small mistakes in the beginning do not spell disaster, but it can be sometimes difficult to get back on track and regain the advantage. If you take the needed time in the beginning to explore and evaluate your business and personal goals, you can then use the information you gain to create a comprehensive, successful business plan that can help you achieve your goals more easily.

The process of developing a solid business plan can force you to process and work through important issues that ordinarily, you may not have considered. The final plan you develop will become a powerful tool as you begin your eBay business.

The purpose of a business plan is to assist you in creating a roadmap that you will need to help you reach your business goals. A business plan also provides you a way to track your progress as you begin and grow your eBay business.

Consider that when you set out on a vacation, you do not begin it by hopping in a car and driving off. To start, you likely decide upon a destination. Then you need a road map to reach your destination. A successful, profitable eBay business is your destination. Your business plan then becomes the road map to reach that destination. A business plan will keep you focused on your journey. It will show you where you are and how far you still need to go. If it is detailed and well thought out, it can also show you the obstacles ahead and ways around them.

Many moneylenders require a complete business plan before they will lend you money. It provides the lender a look at the details of your business and indicates whether you have included a way to pay them back. They want to know that your business is a viable one and that you are a safe investment. If you have gaps or do not take the time necessary to create an outstanding business plan, they may not take the risk of lending the money you need to begin your venture.

A working business plan is likely to be the single most valuable commodity you will ever own. Many initial business plans will just be a bulleted list of goals and the steps necessary to reach them. If you are the only person involved in your eBay business, then you will be the only one reading it for a while. But no matter how many people are involved, a business plan is vital for the success of your company for the following reasons:

- **You**. For you and your coworkers, it will give a list of goals and agendas for the year. A couple of times a year, your business plan should be revisited to see how well you have done and where you need to improve. This will help you make long-term goals and figure out all the monthly, weekly, and daily goals you will need to achieve to reach your ultimate destination. Make sure your eBay business is proceeding in the direction you want it to be going. That way, you will be sure not to quit when times get tough, and you start to run out of steam.

- **Your investors**. The time may come when you want to do something with your business that you do not have the upfront capital to accomplish, and you may decide to look for investors. Suppose you are sure that your business would do well if you could just order those thousands of wine cases from that distributor who is trying to unload a bunch of cases at low prices, but unfortunately, you just do not have the money. Your business plan is something you would show to people who you think should invest in your company. It does not matter whether you are trying to get money from your Uncle Nick, a bank, or some other type of investor, you must have a business plan. Otherwise, you will look sloppy and unprofessional, and people would be right not to invest in you because most likely, you have not thought through what it is going to take for you to accomplish your goal, and for them to get a return on their investments.

Here is a rundown of the elements of a good business plan, and what they will do for your eBay business:

- A business plan is an examination of your products and the way in which you intend to sell them.
- It shows what the market is and who your target audience is.
- It includes a list of your competitors.
- It will show your plan for marketing and sales.
- It will list the costs of doing business.
- If you will have other people working with or under you, your business plan will contain a management plan.
- You will list your finances. You have already begun the process of figuring out what things will cost and what your debt is like.
- Your business plan must outline each activity in detail. It will include timing and constraints.

Next are the various components of a sound business plan. You may use these parts and adapt them to your own needs. You will also find a sample business plan at the end of this book, as well as business plan templates on the CD-ROM that accompanies this book.

Executive Summary

This section of your business plan may be the smallest section, but do not underestimate its importance. This section will summarize who you are, what your company does, where your company is going, and how you are going to get there. When you are trying to secure finances, you may have just a couple of minutes to grab investors' attention. That is why this summary is so important. If it is not eye-catching, and does not contain the necessary information, the investor may not read any further.

Your executive summary must be as thorough as possible while being compelling, and it should entice the reader to read further. This summary must do the following:

- Describe your company
- Describe what your eBay business is and what it offers
- Describe market opportunities

All this must be done in a concise, engaging manner.

Even though your executive summary will appear in the beginning of your business plan, you should create it last. You should write at least a paragraph to describe each section of your completed business plan. You should also finish your executive summary with a listing of the amount of money required to keep your business afloat. Also list major advantages your company will have over the competition.

A well-conceived, complete executive summary will give the reader a quick snapshot of your business, your plans, and what you will need to make it all happen. You should include all your goals and hopes for your eBay business. Your executive summary will capture all the important parts of your plan. Try not to make your summary too long or detailed. Bear in mind that it is just a quick snapshot of the rest of the document. It is meant to grab the readers' attention and leave them wanting to read further. As a rule of thumb, it should be no longer than two pages.

Statement of Purpose

This section describes how this particular business plan is intended to be used. It can be for marketing analysis, to obtain a loan, or to help your business stay focused. It is your choice how the plan will be used; it can be altered later on for different purposes. This is a living document. Its parts are meant to be expanded, changed, and deleted for any purpose you need it for. As your business grows and time passes, you will want to renew your plan to fit your business needs.

Description of the Business

The title to the section is self-explanatory. This section needs to be as detailed as possible. You should describe the who, what, where, why, and how of your eBay business, including the type of products you are selling. This is a synopsis of your business for if you needed to describe your entire operation to someone. It should be tight and neat, while not missing any important details.

History

This history not only includes the history of the business, but your personal business history as well. It should explain how you started your business, and why you started this particular eBay seller business. You can create a schedule of the process of creation, if you like. This section will grow as your business grows. It is an important section, as you can see your business's growth and expansion. This not only helps keep you inspired, but it helps other business associates and lenders see where you came from and what your potential is as a person they are considering doing business with.

Business Name

This section contains your legal name or DBA name. You should also include your Web site names and addresses here.

Business Location

This contains the physical address of your business. You may be working from your home and can include that here. You should also include mailing addresses, if different from your physical address.

Legal Form of Business

This is the type of business your business is considered. Examples are sole proprietorship, LLC, or partnership.

Current Situation

This section looks at the current status of your business, including current financial information, number of clients, the type of formats you are using, successes, failures, and anything else that demonstrates what your eBay business is like at that moment. You should update this at least once a year, if not more often.

The Future and Goals

This section contains goals at the three-month, six-month, one-year, three-year, and five-year marks. You may not know what all these goals should be when you begin. You should list your goals and your objectives, or how you intend to reach the goals you have set for your business. You should have a well-thought-out, detailed plan of how your objectives will manifest your financial and business growth goals. You should include specific dates and definitive amounts of money you wish to earn.

Industry Overview

This section gives a brief overview of the eBay business industry. It can be a generic overview of eBay businesses, or it can be an overview of other businesses that sell the same kinds of products that you do. An example is the collectible PEZ dispenser industry. Information would include how much other eBay businesses are making on average and what the trends are of the industry you have chosen. For instance, if you are selling PEZ dispensers, you might see that there is an increase of people buying Disney PEZ dispensers. This section can be researched online through eBay or other sites that specialize in the types of products you are selling.

Competition

This is a survey of who your competition is. It should include information about your competition and their practices. You can include their Web sites, services, and the total cost of their items. You can also include a comparison of what products they are selling compared to what you currently are offering through eBay.

Major Competitors

From your list of competitors, you should pick the top three. These three should be your toughest competition from among those eBay businesses that are working within or near your niche in your particular market. Go more into depth about their businesses. Also, talk about why your business is different and fills a particular niche. This is a good place to see whether you need to alter the focus of your business a little. If there is just an enormous demographic, then you can hope to compete comfortably with other similar eBay businesses. However, if the customer base is narrow, then you may need to consider changing your niche and offerings. The competitors you list here are the ones you need to watch a little closer. You can add them to your list of sellers and receive notifications of new items they have to offer. If they have a mailing list, be on it. Being aware of what is going on can help keep your business fresh and competitive.

Marketing Strategy

This section deals with how you intend on attracting customers. Will you create a Web site, or perhaps have a large media campaign? Whatever you decide, make sure you add some financial figures about what your plan may cost and how much time you will be spending on marketing. This section is another one that needs to be reviewed and updated on a regular basis. Some marketing strategies will work and others may not. Just be sure you are not pouring money into a strategy that is not producing any results. You must decide when to abandon ship and try a new type of strategy.

Web Site

Many eBay businesses rely heavily on their Web sites. Therefore, you should dedicate a section in your business plan to give an overview of your Web site. This should include what it will look like, what it will contain, whether you are to hire outside help, what the initial cost will be, and what the upkeep will cost you; you can include Web shots of your site, if you like. Your Web site creation may be the most expensive initial startup cost you may incur. Do not skimp on it, as it can mean the difference between the success and failure of your online business.

Income Strategy

You should be figuring and estimating your monthly income here. This will include such items as where your money is coming from, how often you expect to be paid, and what your average costs and profits are on your products. You will need these figures later to add to your cash flow analysis.

Part of your income strategy is savings. Including how you plan to put money aside every month to pay for taxes, insurance, and even retirement. Bear in mind that all these items are up to you now. It is part of owning a small business.

Expert Advice

This is an optional section, though having a PowerSeller as a mentor is not a bad idea. It is in this section that you will talk about your mentor who will help you start up and maintain your eBay business. This can include workshops on eBay business building that you plan to attend or have already attended. Having mentors and other experts helping you will multiply your income and help you through some tough times and situations.

Advertising and Promotion

This is part of your marketing strategy. This section provides much more detail. You will include when you plan to launch your business and what particular media outlets you intend to use. You can even include projections of how you intend to advertise in the future, such as advertisements in magazines, articles online, or even interviews with a variety of media outlets. If you have it in your plan, you are more likely to work toward those goals, rather than just dreaming about it.

Media Objectives and Strategy

This section is optional. Some eBay businesses also have a store connected to them. This section discusses how you intend to approach the media outlets to advertise your online and retail business. Will you send a letter or create a press kit? What will they include? You can even attach your press kit to the business plan. You want this section to be updated as you gain press clippings. If someone else will be in charge of your press and advertising, you should say so in this section.

E-mail

This section is also optional, but you might want to consider using an e-mail address that is easy to recall and unique. Some services require that you use the name of their service in your e-mail address.

eBaypro@hotmail.com is not as memorable as PEZpeople@PEZstore.com.

Having your own domain name may cost a few more dollars a month, but it is worth the cost, as it not only looks more professional, but sets you apart from other fly-by-night operations. Having your own domain name shows that you are serious about your business.

Community

This section can discuss how your business fits within the community. This can be your actual geographical community, or it can be a virtual one. This all depends on the type of business structure you intend on setting up. This section is also the place where you can discuss how you are giving back to the community or doing charitable acts. To truly enmesh yourself within a community, you have to give back to that community.

Operating Procedures

This section deals with the day-to-day procedures of your business. How often are you online? When are you taking photos of products and displaying them on eBay? When do you check and answer e-mails? If you have employees working with you, list them here, and describe what they do. For instance, if you have a marketing person, what are their daily responsibilities? You can be detailed, but you do not have to chart minute-to-minute. Cover all the work that is being done within your business. You can also make a pie chart of your time to see where the majority of your time is being spent. This is important when considering hiring someone to help you, as it can help you determine whether a new person is justified.

Location and Facility

This is the place you are working from. This can also be the place where you are storing your products.

Initial Expenditures

This is the start-up amount needed to get your business up and running. You should include equipment, initial inventory costs, Web site construction, and marketing costs. Try to come up with a total amount, even if you have not finished the process; you can estimate what you think it will cost.

Licenses and Government Regulation

Some places require a business license to do business out of your home. You should also include fees for your DBA permit. If you choose to, you can add the costs of licensing, especially if special licensing is required to set up your eBay business.

Utilities

In this section, you need to try to come up with estimates of what your utilities are and what they cost. This includes phones, Internet service, electric, heat, and any other cost you may be incurring by having a business. In most cases, these will be minimal, unless you are renting a space as an office or a store.

Expenses Budgets

Under this heading, you will include different expenses that you may either incur once or that are ongoing expenses. You should state where the funds for the various items are coming from. Some of the expenses are part of your start-up costs. Other expenses will be part of your monthly expenses and will be paid out as expenses and subtracted from your income. Here are some examples of start-up expenses:

Computer Equipment

- Computer upgrade
- Software
- Scanner
- Copier
- Fax machine

Office Furniture and Supplies

- Large file cabinet
- New phone
- Stationery
- Desk supplies
- Shipping supplies (boxes, bubble wrap, or tape)

Total Initial Expenditures

- Utility deposits
- Computer equipment and software
- Office furniture and supplies

Total Initial Expenditures is the total amount of all your startup expenses.

Personnel and Service

This is a list of your personnel and a short bio of each. You can include a management tree if you like in this section. It may not be necessary, as there are many successful eBay businesses that are one-person operations.

Procedures and Controls

This section will include who is responsible for incoming money and paying any necessary bills. You can have a schedule of bill paying for reoccurring expenses in this section. You should also include any loans you may have and any credit lines associated with your business.

Administrative Salaries

This includes how much you will be paying yourself as the owner of the business. You should keep your finances separate so you do not create any problems for yourself by opening a separate banking account for your business. You should also include how much you are paying others, such as assistants, tax preparers, attorneys, or anyone else you are paying on a regular basis. You may have contract workers, but they are being paid for their services as rendered and do not get a regular salary. If they are receiving a regular salary, you cannot claim they are contract or freelance workers; they then become employees. Be careful, as not paying the appropriate taxes could cost you plenty of money and grief.

Financial Data

This section contains your proposed income, broken down into categories. It includes your products, how much they cost, and how many customers you are projected to be working with. There are many businesses that this may be tough to do with because the products may be different every day. Do your best to estimate the average cost of your items.

One thing that makes eBay unique is the bidding structure. You never know exactly how much you might get for an item. There are controls for this, such as minimum bids, buy now options, and reserves. If you are starting out with your eBay business, this may be difficult to estimate. Since this is a guide for advanced sellers, it is assumed that you have been selling your items for a period of time, and therefore, estimation may be easier.

You can make growth projections based upon the market by monitoring your competition's sales and number of items they are selling. All this information is easy to obtain by looking at their profiles.

You have gathered your expenses and projected salary, so make sure that your projected sales take all those expenses into account. You may find that you need to lower your salary a bit the first couple of years and try to save on expenses wherever you can.

You can do a four- or five-year projection like the one that follows. The first column is your gross income before taxes, and the second is your net income. Take note that you have to deposit money aside every month to pay for taxes. You must figure this in as a weekly or biweekly expense. The Internal Revenue Service (IRS) requires that you show proof of deposit into an account to be paid at tax time. Failure to do this can result in fines.

Year	Gross Revenue	Net Income After Taxes
Year 1	$10,250	-$1,930
Year 2	$14,160	$12,204
Year 3	$18,675	$16,620
Year 4	$23,889	$21,731

Capital Requirements

Once you have determined what the amount of your start-up costs are going to be, you will put that amount in this section. You should add your equipment costs, and other costs will be from the previous section. You should then double this amount to have money in the account to help you through the first few months of operation, until you begin to have a cash flow. Some small business owners keep their full-time jobs and start slowly until they have built up a sufficient customer base. This is a smart idea if you do not have a large enough capital to begin with.

Conclusion

In the conclusion of your plan, you will determine, using all the available information and financial data, whether your plan to begin an eBay business is viable. It could mean that you need to wait until you can either borrow or save more capital. It could also mean that you need to do more research. If you have purchased this book, then you have already decided that you want to continue your eBay business. You can use this area to determine what you need to do to accelerate your business and become a PowerSeller. You may need to work on your service plan and develop a good Web site. Whatever the case, allow your analytical mind to make the choice. When it comes to money, you cannot allow your desires and emotions to overcome reason and numbers. This is not to say you should not take chances. What it does mean is that you need to make smart choices and take educated risks.

Monthly Balance Sheet

As you begin to monitor your income and expenses, you will want to fill out a monthly balance sheet. This is especially important when trying to make your business grow. It provides an excellent analysis of how your business is fairing and gives a template in which you can see strengths and weaknesses of your business and marketing plan.

Some of the expenses in the sample may apply to you and some may not. You can add or remove income and expense items. You should change them to work for your particular financial situation.

Sample Balance Sheet

		Aug-08	Sept-08	Oct-08	Nov-08	Dec-08	Jan-09	Feb-09	Mar-09	Apr-09	May-09	Jun-09	Jul-09
Current Assets													
Cash	$2,600	$1,103	($587)	($596)	($797)	($890)	($975)	($1049)	($1,112)	($1,163)	($1,200)	($1,223)	
Investments	$0	$0	$0	$0	$0	$0	$0	$0	$0	$0	$0	$0	
Inventory	$0	$0	$0	$0	$0	$0	$0	$0	$0	$0	$0	$0	
Other Current Assets													
Total Current Assets	$3,500	$2,003	($587)	($596)	($697)	($790)	($875)	($949)	($1,012)	($1,063)	($1,100)	($1,123)	
Fixed Assets													
Building/Leasehold													
Improvements	$0	$0	$0	$0	$0	$0	$0	$0	$0	$0	$0	$0	
Computer Equipment	$1,500	$1,500	$1,500	$1,500	$1,500	$1,500	$1,500	$1,500	$1,500	$1,500	$1,500	$1,500	
Furniture	$1,000	$1,000	$1,000	$1,000	$1,000	$1,000	$1,000	$1,000	$1,000	$1,000	$1,000	$1,000	
Less Accumulated Depreciation	$1012	($12)	($36)	($60)	($84)	($108)	($132)	($156)	($180)	($204)	($228)	($252)	
Total Fixed Assets	$2,512	$2,488	$2,464	$2,440	$2,416	$2,392	$2,368	$2,344	$2,320	$2,296	$2,272	$2,248	
Total Current Assets	$5,112	$3,591	$2,076	$2,943	$1,818	$1,701	$1,592	$1,494	$1,407	$1,332	$1,271	$1,224	
Liabilities													
Current Liabilities													
Short-Term Debt	$0	$0	$0	$0	$0	$0	$0	$0	$0	$0	$0	$0	
Accounts Payable	$0	$0	$0	$0	$0	$0	$0	$0	$0	$0	$0	$0	

Notes Payable/Mortgage	$0	$0	$0	$0	$0	$0	$0	$0	$0	$0	$0	$0	
Other Payables	$0	$0	$0	$0	$0	$0	$0	$0	$0	$0	$0	$0	
Accrued Liabilities													
Total Current Liabilities													
Long-Term Debt	$0	$0	$0	$0	$0	$0	$0	$0	$0	$0	$0	$0	
Total Liabilities	$0	$0	$0	$0	$0	$0	$0	$0	$0	$0	$0	$0	
Owner Equity													
Owner's Equity	$0	$0	$0	$0	$0	$0	$0	$0	$0	$0	$0	$0	
Retained Earnings	$0	$0	$0	$0	$0	$0	$0	$0	$0	$0	$0	$0	
Net Income/(Loss)	($1,496)	($1,490)	($108)	($101)	($93)	($84)	($74)	($63)	($51)	($37)	($23)	($7)	
Total Owner's Equity	$3,515	$2,000	$1,867	$1,742	$1,625	$1,516	$1,418	$1,331	$1,256	$1,195	$1,148	$1,117	
Total Liabilities and Equity	$2,018	$509	$1,758	$1,640	$1,531	$1,432	$1,344	$1,268	$1,205	$1,157	$1,124	$1,110	

Break-Even Analysis

The next financial analysis is your break-even analysis. This is the point at which your expenses and income are equal. You need to at least make this point, but always strive to tip the scales toward more income than expenses. You should look at this break-even point at least yearly, but in the beginning, you should follow this more closely. If you find yourself not making your break-even point, you have two options — increase your income or decrease your expenses. You need to figure out where you can increase your sales or be more efficient with your resources. As with the monthly balance sheet, the break-even analysis that follows may not contain all the applicable fields for your particular situation. Do what you need to customize it to your business.

In the sample, you will notice two main categories — fixed and variable costs. Fixed costs are those that do not generally change from month to month, and if they do, it is minimal and usually due to added fees. Variable fees are those that often change month to month. These are fees like electric or cell phone bills. These are harder to gauge in a break-even analysis, as these will change the final number slightly month to month. You can do an average over a few months or a year to get a better idea. The longer that you record your finances, the better an idea you will have about what they will be.

You will notice that some of the line items are in brackets, and there are no figures for the year. These are items that you may not be paying for or that are not applicable to your particular situation. I have left them there for illustrative purposes.

Break-Even Analysis Sample

	Aug-08	Sept-08	Oct-08	Nov-08	Dec-08	Jan-09	Feb-09	Mar-09	Apr-09	May-09	June-09	July-09	Aug-09
Fixed Costs													
Operating Expenses													
Accounting/Payroll Processing	$0	$0	$0	$0	$0	$0	$0	$0	$0	$0	$0	$0	$0
Administrative Salaries	$0	$0	$0	$0	$0	$0	$0	$0	$0	$0	$0	$0	$0
Administrative Office Expenses	$1,025	$125	$125	$125	$125	$125	$125	$125	$125	$125	$125	$125	$1,300
Advertising and Promotions	$400	$400	$200	$200	$200	$200	$200	$200	$200	$200	$200	$200	$1,700
Bank Fees	$7	$7	$7	$7	$7	$7	$7	$7	$7	$7	$7	$7	$95
(Insurance)	$0	$0	$0	$0	$0	$0	$0	$0	$0	$0	$0	$0	$0
(Exterminator)	$0	$0	$0	$0	$0	$0	$0	$0	$0	$0	$0	$0	$0
(Legal Fees)	$0	$0	$0	$0	$0	$0	$0	$0	$0	$0	$0	$0	$0
(Licenses and Permits)	$50	$0	$0	$0	$0	$0	$0	$0	$0	$0	$0	$0	$50
(Payroll Staff)	$0	$0	$0	$0	$0	$0	$0	$0	$0	$0	$0	$0	$0
(Lease Payment)	$0	$0	$0	$0	$0	$0	$0	$0	$0	$0	$0	$0	$0
Repairs and Maintenance	$0	$0	$0	$0	$0	$0	$0	$0	$0	$0	$0	$0	$0
(Trash Removal)	$0	$0	$0	$0	$0	$0	$0	$0	$0	$0	$0	$0	$0
(Real Estate Taxes)	$0	$0	$0	$0	$0	$0	$0	$0	$0	$0	$0	$0	$0

(Payroll Taxes)	$0	$0	$0	$0	$0	$0	$0	$0	$0	$0	$0	$0	$0
(Telephone/Internet)	$25	$25	$25	$25	$25	$25	$25	$25	$25	$25	$25	$25	$311.00
(Utilities)	$0	$0	$0	$0	$0	$0	$0	$0	$0	$0	$0	$0	$0
(Worker's Compensation)	$0	$0	$0	$0	$0	$0	$0	$0	$0	$0	$0	$0	$0
Total Fixed Cost	$1,507	$557	$357	$357	$357	$357	$357	$357	$357	$357	$357	$357	$3,456
Variable Costs													
(Professional Fees/Other)	$100	$0	$0	$0	$0	$0	$0	$0	$0	$0	$0	$0	$100
Paper Supplies	$150	$25	$25	$25	$25	$25	$25	$25	$25	$25	$25	$25	$425
Total Variable Costs	$250	$25	$25	$25	$25	$25	$25	$25	$25	$25	$25	$25	$525
Total Fixed plus Variable Costs	$2007	$607	$407	$407	$407	$407	$407	$407	$407	$407	$407	$407	$4506
Income from Operations	$62	$68	$75	$82	$90	$99	$109	$120	$132	$146	$160	$176	$1,325
Contribution Margin	-303%	63%	66%	69%	72%	74%	77%	79%	81%	82%	84%	85%	60%
Break-Even Sales Volume	($431)	$566	$238	$227	$219	$211	$205	$200	$195	$191	$188	$185	$5,391
Sales Volume Above Break-Even	$493	($498)	($163)	($145)	($128)	($112)	($95)	($79)	($62)	($45)	($27)	($8)	($4,066)

Monthly Income Projection

Based upon your sales or other sources of income, your income projection is an analysis of how your marketing efforts are paying off. You can make this table more accurate by surveying your clients to determine how they learned about your products; keep a log of this information. This projection will help you determine where your sources of income are coming from and whether your marketing budget is being spent in the right areas.

Some of the areas will be relevant to your eBay business and some will not. You will be able to see where the percentage of your money is being used. In the example, the cost of running the business is more than the revenue being made. Upon analysis, there are areas that are costing too much and can be cut back to at least get to a break-even point, but the goal is to make it well past that point. While you may be a "PowerSeller," you may not be making a dime because your costs are too high. Throughout this book, you will find tips for streamlining the process to correct any problems that will stand in the way of profits.

Monthly Income Projection Sample

	Aug-08	Sept-08	Oct-08	Nov-08	Dec-08	Jan-09	Feb-09	Mar-09	Apr-09	May-09	Jun-09	Jul-09	Year	% of total sales
REVENUE														
Advertisements	$17	$18	$20	$22	$24	$27	$30	$33	$36	$40	$44	$48	$363	27%
Affiliate Sales (from reviews)	$25	$27	$30	$33	$36	$40	$44	$48	$53	$58	$64	$71	$534	40%
Affiliate Sales (from virtual store)	$20	$22	$24	$26	$29	$32	$35	$38	$42	$47	$51	$57	$427	32%
Total Revenue	$62	$68	$75	$82	$90	$99	$109	$120	$132	$146	$160	$176	$1,325	100%
COST OF REVENUE														
Advertisements	$20	$20	$20	$20	$20	$20	$20	$20	$20	$20	$20	$20	$20	100%
Affiliate Sales (from reviews)	$0	$0	$0	$0	$0	$0	$0	$0	$0	$0	$0	$0	$0	0%

Affiliate Sales (from virtual store)	$0	$0	$0	$0	$0	$0	$0	$0	$0	$0	$0	$0	$0	0%
Total Cost of														
Goods Sold	$0	$0	$0	$0	$0	$0	$0	$0	$0	$0	$0	$0	$0	0%
% of total sales	0%	0%	0%	0%	0%	0%	0%	0%	0%	0%	0%	0%	0%	
Gross Profit	$62	$68	$75	$82	$90	$99	$109	$120	$132	$146	$160	$176	$1,325	100%
% of total sales	100%	100%	100%	100%	100%	100%	100%	100%	100%	100%	100%	100%	100%	
Operating Expenses														
(without depreciation)	$1,558	$383	$183	$183	$183	$183	$183	$183	$183	$183	$183	$183	$3,781	285%
Depreciation	$0	$0	$0	$0	$0	$0	$0	$0	$0	$0	$0	$0	$0	0%
Total Operating														
Expenses	$1,558	$1,558	$183	$183	$183	$183	$183	$183	$183	$183	$183	$183	$3,781	$2
% of total sales	2,514%	2,285%	245%	222%	202%	184%	167%	152%	138%	125%	114%	103%	285%	
Income from														
Operations	($1,496)	($1,490)	($108)	($101)	($93)	($84)	($74)	($63)	($51)	($37)	($23)	($7)	($3,630)	-273%

% of total sales	-2,414%	-2,185%	-145%	-122%	-102%	-84%	-67%	-52%	-38%	-25%	-14%	-3%	-273%	
Taxes on Income	$0	$0	$0	$0	$0	$0	$0	$0	$0	$0	$0	$0	$0	0%
% of total sales	0%	0%	0%	0%	0%	0%	0%	0%	0%	0%	0%	0%	0%	
Net Income After Taxes	($1,496)	($1,490)	($108)	($101)	($93)	($84)	($74)	($63)	($51)	($37)	($23)	($7)	($3,630)	-273%
% of total sales	-2,414%	-2,185%	-145%	-122%	-102%	-84%	-67%	-52%	-38%	-25%	-14%	-3%	-273%	

Cash-Flow Summary

The next set of tables is your cash-flow summary. This is a holistic look at your financial situation. You have made projections and know what your break-even point is. Here, you will be able to see how you are doing. It is here that you can determine whether you are on a leaky boat. You can see whether you are saving money and growing your company or just living month by month.

You should look hard at this table and determine how long you should give your business a try before giving up or restructuring — the numbers never lie. You cannot rely on what you want or can make; you have to rely on what you are making. You can only sacrifice so much before you are dipping into your personal expenses. It is at this point that you need to look hard at the viability of your business. It is better to fail at a business and get out than to lose your life savings and worry about your mortgage. This is why consulting with an eBay expert or having another PowerSeller helping you can be quite valuable. They can help you assess your situation and can point out places to work on before it is too late. If they are to be effective in helping you, they will be brutally honest and suggest you shift your business before you hit rock bottom.

There is a difference between making a profit and being able to make a living. In the sample I have given you, the person is making a profit, but not nearly enough to be making a decent living. While it is important to keep your personal finances from your business ones, there is a direct connection between the two. This occurs because you are running your own business. If you are not creating enough income to cover your personal expenses, then you will not be able to last very long. You need to be at a point of "paying" yourself a wage. This separates your personal finances from the business. Do not use business finances to pay your car payment. One of the first orders of business, if you have not already done so, is to open up a separate bank account for your business.

Cash-Flow Summary: Years One through Five Sample

For the year ending	July-2008	July-2009	July-2010	July-2011	July-2012
CASH FROM OPERATIONS					
Advertisements	$363	$1,140	$2,378	$3,808	$6,096
Affiliate Sales (from reviews)	$534	$1,677	$3,498	$5,600	$8,967
Affiliate Sales (from virtual store)	$427	$1,342	$2,798	$4,480	$7,173
TOTAL REVENUES	$1,325	$4,160	$8,675	$13,889	$22,237
Cash Available from Financing					
Owner's Investment	$5,000	$0	$0	$0	$0
Mortgage	$0	$0	$0	$0	$0
Change in Accounts Payable	$0	$0	$0	$0	$0
Long-Term Loan Proceeds	$0	$0	$0	$0	$0
Short-Term Loan Proceeds	$0	$0	$0	$0	$0
Sale of Investments	$0	$0	$0	$0	$0
Sale of Other Current Assets	$0	$0	$0	$0	$0
Sale of Other Assets	$0	$0	$0	$0	$0

Cash Available from Financing	$5,000	$0	$0	$0	$0
Total Cash Available	$6,325	$4,160	$8,675	$13,889	$22,237
CASH DISBURSEMENTS					
COSTS OF GOODS SOLD					
Advertisements	$0	$0	$0	$0	$0
Affiliate Sales (from reviews)	$0	$0	$0	$0	$0
Affiliate Sales (from virtual store)	$0	$0	$0	$0	$0
Total Cost of Goods Sold	$0	$0	$0	$0	$0
Accounting/Payroll Processing	$0	$0	$0	$0	$0
Administrative Salaries	$0	$0	$0	$0	$0
Administrative Office Expenses	$1,200	$300	$315	$330	$347
Advertising and Promotions	$1,600	$1,200	$1,260	$1,323	$1,389
Bank Fees	$95	$95	$100	$105	$110
Insurance	$0	$0	$0	$0	$0
Exterminator	$0	$0	$0	$0	$0

Legal Fees	$0	$0	$0	$0	$0
Licenses and Permits	$50	$50	$52	$55	$57
Royalty Fees	$0	$0	$0	$0	$0
Payroll Staff	$0	$0	$0	$0	$0
Lease Payment	$0	$0	$0	$0	$0
Repairs and Maintenance	$0	$0	$0	$0	$0
Trash Removal	$0	$0	$0	$0	$0
Real Estate Taxes	$0	$0	$0	$0	$0
Payroll Taxes	$0	$0	$0	$0	$0
Telephone/Internet	$311	$311	$326	$343	$360
Utilities	$0	$0	$0	$0	$0
Worker's Compensation	$0	$0	$0	$0	$0
Total Operating Expenses	$3,256	$1,956	$2,054	$2,157	$2,265
OTHER APPLICATIONS OF CASH					
Land	$0	$0	$0	$0	$0
Buildings	$0	$0	$0	$0	$0
Leasehold Improvements	$0	$0	$0	$0	$0
Computer Equipment	$850	$0	$0	$0	$0
Furniture	$225	$0	$0	$0	$0

Change in Inventory	$0	$0	$0	$0	$0
Purchase of Other Current Assets	$0	$0	$0	$0	$0
Purchase of Other Assets	$0	$0	$0	$0	$0
Purchase of Investments	$0	$0	$0	$0	$0
Dividends Payable	$0	$0	$0	$0	$0
TOTAL OTHER APPLICATIONS	$1,075	$0	$0	$0	$0
TOTAL CASH-OUTLAY	$4,331	$1,956	$2,054	$2,157	$2,265
BEGINNING MONTH CASH BALANCE	$2,500	$1,994	$2,204	$6,620	$11,731
ENDING MONTH CASH BALANCE	$1,994	$2,204	$6,620	$11,731	$19,972

If you look closely at the cash-flow analysis sample, you can see that there were some years that were better than others. If you look at it as a whole, though, you will see a steady increase in cash flow. Do not be discouraged by a month or two, or even a slightly less profitable year. You have to look at the numbers in a wider spectrum, which is why it is recommended that you compare more than one year.

Tips from the Experts

Keeping my costs down and buying right are my secrets. I'm a firm believer that you make your money when you buy your inventory. Don't buy inventory on emotion. Run the numbers first, and make sure the profit potential is there.

— Tom Orr

Operating Budget

The next set of tables looks at the operating budget. This is the cost of doing business. This is all the everyday expenses broken down, and it provides an analysis of areas in which you could cut back. For instance, if your Web hosting is costing you $100 a month, and you find a different service for $30, that can be a savings of $840 a year. For someone who is running a small business, $840 a year is significant. It can mean a new computer or more inventory.

Operating Budget Summary: Years One through Five Sample

For the year ending	July-08	July-09	July-10	July-11	July-12
Sales					
Advertisements	$363	$1,140	$2,378	$3,808	$6,096
Affiliate Sales (from reviews)	$534	$1,677	$3,498	$5,600	$8,967
Affiliate Sales (from virtual store)	$427	$1,342	$2,798	$4,480	$7,173
Total Sales	$1,325	$4,160	$8,675	$13,889	$22,237
Cost of Sales					
Advertisements	$0	$0	$0	$0	$0
Affiliate Sales (from reviews)	$0	$0	$0	$0	$0
Affiliate Sales (from virtual store)	$0	$0	$0	$0	$0
Total Cost of Goods Sold	$0	$0	$0	$0	$0
% of Total Sales	0%	0%	0%	0%	0%
Gross Profits	$1,325	$4,160	$8,675	$13,889	$22,237

% of Total Sales	100%	100%	100%	100%	100%
Operating Expenses					
Accounting/Payroll Processing	$0	$0	$0	$0	$0
Administrative Salaries	$0	$0	$0	$0	$0
Administrative Office Expenses	$1,200	$300	$315	$330	$347
Advertising and Promotions	$1,600	$1,200	$1,260	$1,323	$1,389
Bank Fees	$95	$95	$100	$105	$110
Insurance	$0	$0	$0	$0	$0
Exterminator	$0	$0	$0	$0	$0
Legal Fees	$0	$0	$0	$0	$0
Licenses and Permits	$50	$50	$52	$55	$57
Royalty Fees	$0	$0	$0	$0	$0
Payroll Staff	$0	$0	$0	$0	$0
Lease Payment	$0	$0	$0	$0	$0
Repairs and Maintenance	$0	$0	$0	$0	$0
Trash Removal	$0	$0	$0	$0	$0
Real Estate Taxes	$0	$0	$0	$0	$0
Payroll Taxes	$0	$0	$0	$0	$0
Telephone/Internet	$311	$311	$326	$343	$360
Utilities	$0	$0	$0	$0	$0
Worker's Compensation	$0	$0	$0	$0	$0

Total Operating Expenses	$3,256	$1,956	$2,054	$2,157	$2,265
% of Total Sales	245%	47%	23%	15%	10%
Total Expenses	$3,256	$1,956	$2,054	$2,157	$2,265
% of Total Sales	245%	47%	23%	15%	10%
Net Profit Before Income Tax	($1,930)	$2,204	$6,620	$11,731	$19,972
% of Total Sales	-145%	52%	76%	84%	89%
Taxes on Income	$0	$661	$1,986	$3,519	$5,991
% of Total Sales	0%	15%	22%	25%	26%
Net Income After Taxes	($1,930)	$1,542	$4,634	$8,212	$13,980
% of Total Sales	-145%	37%	53%	59%	62%

Income Statements

In the next set of tables, you will be able to see what your actual income was. You can compare this to your earlier projections. Are the numbers close? If not, what caused the discrepancy? Was there something you missed or did not count on? Has there been a shift in the industry? These tables can help you analyze these questions and make necessary changes.

Income Statements Summary: Years One through Five Sample

	Year 1	Year 2	Year 3	Year 4	Year 5
REVENUE					
Advertisements	$363	$1,140	$2,378	$3,808	$6,096
Affiliate Sales (from reviews)	$534	$1,677	$3,498	$5,600	$8,967
Affiliate Sales (from virtual store)	$427	$1,342	$2,798	$4,480	$7,173
Total Revenue	$1,325	$4,160	$8,675	$13,889	$22,237
COST OF REVENUE					
Advertisements	$0	$0	$0	$0	$0
Affiliate Sales (from reviews)	$0	$0	$0	$0	$0
Affiliate Sales (from virtual store)	$0	$0	$0	$0	$0
Total Cost of					
Goods Sold	$0	$0	$0	$0	$0
% of total sales	0	0	0	0	0
Gross Profit	$1,325	$4,160	$8,675	$13,889	$22,237
% of total sales					
Operating Expenses					
(without depreciation)	$3,781	$2,481	$2,684	$2,906	$3,151

Depreciation	$0	$0	$0	$0	$0
Total Operating					
Expenses	$3,781	$2,481	$2,684	$2,906	$3,151
% of total sales	0	0	0	0	0
Income from					
Operations	-$3,630	$1,679	$5,991	$10,982	$19,085
% of total sales	-2	0	0	0	0
Taxes on Income	$0	$0	$0	$0	$0
% of total sales	0	0	0	0	0
Net Income After Taxes	-$3,630	$1,679	$5,991	$10,982	$19,085
% of total sales	-273%	40%	69%	79%	85%

CHAPTER 16

Evaluating the Success of Your Business

Tips from the Experts

I once bought a stack of eight art magazines at a garage sale (and I rarely go to garage sales) for $1 and sold them for almost $150 on eBay. I knew what they were worth, as I had to replace my set of those same magazines when I moved from Wyoming to Hawaii and they were lost in transit.

— Charlene Anderson

Evaluating Your Success after Six Months

One way to evaluate how your business is doing and determine how to improve it is called a SWOT analysis. SWOT stands for Strengths, Weaknesses, Opportunities, and Threats.

Your strengths and weaknesses are determined in reference to your competition and others in the industry, not based upon your own history. Strengths and weaknesses are internal to your eBay selling business. Opportunities and threats are from external sources, such as your competition. These competitors should be current and new arrivals on eBay. You can research on eBay and determine who your closest competition is.

Using a SWOT analysis will help you focus your energy on areas where you are the strongest and concentrate on where the greatest opportunities are.

How to do a SWOT Analysis

The first thing you will consider is your business strengths. I have included a worksheet here that can also be found on the CD. Here are some things to consider as you fill out this worksheet:

- What sets your service apart in the industry?
- What does your business do well?
- What resources and suppliers do you have to work with?
- What do your clients say your company's strengths are? (You can get this information from sending them an evaluation of your service. See the next section for examples).

When you fill your worksheet out, make sure you are honest, and do not be modest. Put items in there that make your company shine.

Worksheet SWOT: Strengths

On this worksheet, make sure you are adding your company's internal strengths and what sets your company apart from other eBay business. You should think about other businesses that are close to your niche of products you are selling. You can add as many strengths as you wish. When you are done, figure out what your top eight strengths are.

Your company's strengths	Description of the strengths (Be clear and concise)	Ways to continue to build on those strengths

The next thing you will evaluate is your company's weaknesses. As you fill out the weakness, here are some questions to help you through the process.

- What are things that can improve in your business?
- What does your business not do as well as you would like?
- What things have your clients said need improvement in your company? (Again, this can be drawn from comments or a survey done with them after you have completed your service with them)
- Is your competition doing better than you are?

As with the strengths, you want to be honest. No one needs to see this list but you, so put it all out there.

Worksheet SWOT: Weaknesses

On this worksheet, you are going to list the weaknesses of your eBay business. These can be deficiencies in the area of resources or capabilities of your company. These are items that do not enable you to follow your mission and values statements during the course of doing business. You may add as many weaknesses as you wish. When you are done, determine your eight highest priority weaknesses.

Your company's weaknesses	Description of the weaknesses	Ways you can lessen the impact or eliminate your weaknesses

Opportunities are from external sources. As you fill out your opportunities worksheet, consider using the following questions:

- Where are the best opportunities for your company?
- What are the new trends in eBay and your niche industry?
- Where can you find these new trends?
- Are there changes in the market that can improve your business?
- Are there new vendors or venues to be considered?
- Are there trade shows or places you can find new clients?

You can look at your strengths list and consider what and where the opportunities are that can help you bolster your strengths. You can also look at your weaknesses list and consider where you might find ways to eliminate some of these weaknesses.

Worksheet SWOT: Opportunities

On this worksheet, you are considering outside factors and people that can improve and help your eBay business. You can list as many opportunities on your sheet as you like. When you are done, compare them to your vision statement, value statement, and any other component in your business plan. See whether they resonate with one another. You may have to adjust your plan or your opportunity to make sure you are placing your focus on the right items. When you have completed your changes, come up with a plan to implement using your opportunities.

Your company's opportunities	Descriptions of those opportunities	Action plan for using those opportunities

The last component of your SWOT analysis is threats. These are external threats and should not be confused with weaknesses. Here are some questions to help you fill out your threats worksheet.

- What obstacles does your business face?

- What is your competition doing that is affecting your company?
- Are there any regulations or laws that have changed about operating an eBay business?
- Is your company facing financial or debt problems?

Worksheet SWOT: Threats

On this worksheet, you will be listing situations, people, and factors that affect your eBay business negatively. You may list as many factors as you wish. Decide which factors are in your control and which ones are not. Come up with a plan to try to reduce or eliminate threats that you have control over.

Your company's threats	Descriptions of those threats	Action plan for eliminating the threat or lessening its impact upon your company

Surveys

When you have completed doing business with a customer, it is always nice to send them a thank-you e-mail, or you can mail a letter. In it, you can send a short survey designed to help your company.

The survey should be brief. Keep a tally of the number of returned surveys to see whether this is a good marketing strategy for you.

Following is a sample thank-you letter and a sample survey:

PEZ KING
123 Main Street
Anywhere, USA

August 18, 2008
Mr. PEZ Collector
456 N Main Street
Anywhere, USA

Dear Mr. Collector:

On behalf of everyone at PEZ KING, thank you for choosing us to provide you with the most exciting PEZ collectibles.

We are committed to our customers to provide them the highest level of customer satisfaction possible. If for any reason you have questions or comments, we are delighted to hear from you. Call us at 1-800-555-1234, or send us an e-mail at PEZ@service.com. You can expect us to respond to your e-mail within 24 hours.

Our company relies on the generosity of you, our customers, in spreading the word about our superb PEZ Collection products. So please visit our eBay store and tell your friends and family. Mention this e-mail and get 10% off of your next order.

In addition, I have included a quick survey. It takes less than five minutes to fill out and send back. Please be honest and add any comments that we can use to improve the way we do business. If you would like to add positive comments, we would love to use them on our Web site and promotional materials.

Again, thank you for your patronage. We hope you think of us for your future PEZ purchases.

Sincerely,

Loreena PEZ

Tips from the Experts

Get involved with eBay Giving Works! List an item at least once a month 100% to charity, and have several items each month with at least a percentage to a nonprofit of your choice. Selling on the eBay Giving Works platform has advantages besides helping a great organization; it can help your business.

— Danna Crawford

Sample Survey

PEZ KING Survey

Please fill out the following survey. Circle the number that most closely represents your answer. 1 is strongly agree, 2 is agree, 3 is no opinion, 4 is disagree, 5 is strongly disagree. When you are finished, please fold this paper in half with the address label and stamp on the outside and mail it back to us. You can staple or tape the ends firmly. Thank you for your time and generosity.

Please Rate the following:	1	2	3	4	5
PEZ King filled my order quickly					
Payment was easy					
PEZ King offered other products I was interested in					
I will recommend Loreena to friends and family for their PEZ purchases					
PEZ King had competitive prices					
Shipping was quick					
Shipping was reasonably priced					
I was able to navigate PEZ King's Web site easily					
(If applicable) Customer service was helpful and solved my issues					
I will shop at PEZ King again					

How to Look at Success after One Year

When you reach the one-year mark, it is time to look at where you have been, where you are, and where you want to go. If you did not already do a SWOT analysis, or want to do another one, now is a good time.

In addition, you should send out surveys to your vendors and suppliers. These are similar to the ones you would send to clients, and these also provide feedback about the strengths and weaknesses of your company.

It is at the one-year mark that you have to do some honest soul searching. Does your eBay business have what it takes to succeed? The money you are making should not be the only component used to determine whether your business is viable. It can take a few years to get any small business to make a profit. You do want to at least break even. You may be worrying about how to keep the lights on at home. If so, you may need to work a part-time job until your business can turn a profit.

A steady stream of successful auctions is a better indication of success. Depending on what you are selling, your eBay business may have more profitable seasons. You should keep a calendar for the year and look at when you sold the mot products to use as a guide. Sales can change slightly from year to year, but you should find that they follow a predictable pattern.

Tips from the Experts

Guts; self-motivation; $400; a desire to succeed; and curiosity to learn everything I could about my products, about eBay, about the Web, about HTML, and about business in general were the things I needed to become a successful eBay seller.

— Charlene Anderson

Projected Profit and Loss

An example of projected profit and loss is shown in the following table. This chart looks at what you are making in sales and what the cost of doing business is. When the amount is below the break-even point, you are having a loss. When you are above the break-even point, you are making a profit. The net profit is the actual amount of profit you are making.

Profit and Loss of the PEZ Kings

For the year ending	July-07	July-08	July-09	July-10	July-11
Sales					
Advertisements	$363	$1140	$2378	$3808	$6096
Affiliate Sales (from reviews)	$534	$1677	$3498	$5600	$8967
Affiliate Sales (from virtual store)	$427	$1342	$2798	$4480	$7173
Total Sales	$1325	$4160	$8675	$13889	$22237
Cost of Sales					
Advertisements	$0	$0	$0	$0	$0
Affiliate Sales (from reviews)	$0	$0	$0	$0	$0
Affiliate Sales (from virtual store)	$0	$0	$0	$0	$0
Total Cost of Goods Sold	$0	$0	$0	$0	$0
% of Total Sales	0%	0%	0%	0%	0%
Gross Profits	$1325	$4160	$8675	$13889	$22237
% of Total Sales	100%	100%	100%	100%	100%
Operating Expenses					
Accounting/Payroll Processing	$0	$0	$0	$0	$0
Administrative Salaries	$0	$0	$0	$0	$0
Administrative Office Expenses	$1200	$300	$315	$330	$347
Advertising and Promotions	$1600	$1200	$1260	$1323	$1389
Bank Fees	$95	$95	$100	$105	$110
Insurance	$0	$0	$0	$0	$0

Exterminator	$0	$0	$0	$0	$0
Legal Fees	$0	$0	$0	$0	$0
Licenses and Permits	$50	$50	$52	$55	$57
Royalty Fees	$0	$0	$0	$0	$0
Payroll Staff	$0	$0	$0	$0	$0
Lease Payment	$0	$0	$0	$0	$0
Repairs and Maintenance	$0	$0	$0	$0	$0
Trash Removal	$0	$0	$0	$0	$0
Real Estate Taxes	$0	$0	$0	$0	$0
Payroll Taxes	$0	$0	$0	$0	$0
Telephone/Internet	$311	$311	$326	$343	$360
Utilities	$0	$0	$0	$0	$0
Worker's Compensation	$0	$0	$0	$0	$0
Total Operating Expenses	$3256	$1956	$2054	$2157	$2265
% of Total Sales	245%	47%	23%	15%	10%
Total Expenses	$3256	$1956	$2054	$2157	$2265
% of Total Sales	245%	47%	23%	15%	10%
Net Profit Before Income Tax	($1930)	$2204	$6620	$11731	$19972
% of Total Sales	-145%	52%	76%	84%	89%
Taxes on Income	$0	$661	$1986	$3519	$5991
% of Total Sales	0%	15%	22%	25%	26%
Net Income After Taxes	($1930)	$1542	$4634	$8212	$13980
% of Total Sales	-145%	37%	53%	59%	62%

Profit Monthly

You can look at and chart your monthly profits if you do not want to wait a year. In addition, you can look at what months you are making the most money and when you are not making as much. The months when profits are lower, you can concentrate on other aspects of your business, such as marketing. You can do research, see what items are selling well on eBay, and decide whether you need to shift your inventory to keep up with the changing market.

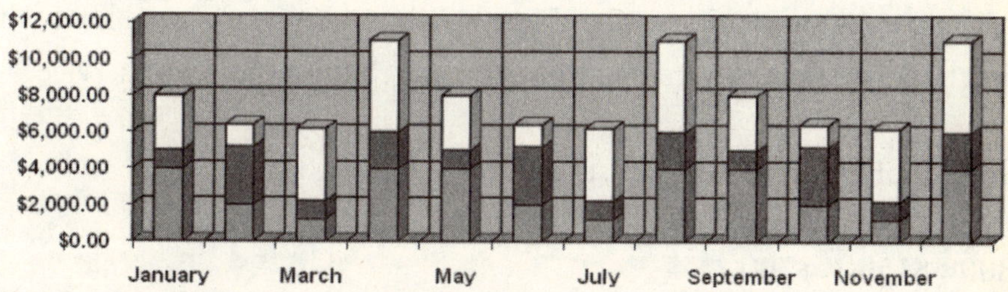

Profit Yearly

You can use these charts to look at your business at the three-year mark, or even expand this into a five-year mark. You should see your profits rise over three to five years. These charts help you predict what the following year's profits should be.

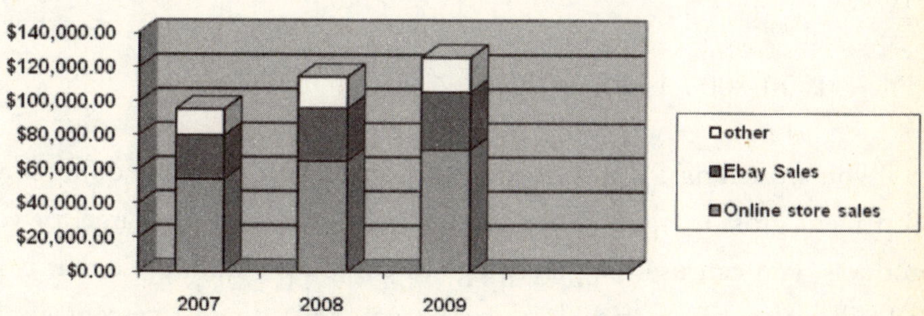

Gross Margin Monthly

Gross margin is the amount of contribution to your business after you have paid for fixed and variable costs and the amount needed to cover overheads. Suppose it costs you a certain amount to sell products on eBay with the cost of phone calls, Internet expenses, or storage. This is important because if you charge $1,500 and you spent $700 in materials and expenses, then your gross margin would be $800. You would need to increase your price to cover your costs so that you will know exactly what you are making. Here are some equations to help you determine your gross margin. The first helps you determine exactly how much money you are making when you charge a price. Revenue is what you are charging for your service.

Gross Profit = Revenue – Cost Of Doing Business

$800= $1500- $700

To calculate your gross margin in terms of percentage, you would use the following equation. It is important to see the percentage of what you are charging and what you are actually making. You do not want to be charging too little and not making enough money.

Gross Margin Percentage = (Revenue - Cost of Doing Business / Revenue) x 100

53% = (1500-700 / 1500) x 100

So if you are selling $1,500 worth of products, you are really doing it at a 53 percent gross margin. When calculating how much to charge for your products, you can use the percentage to come up with a price that is fair and still makes you money. In this case, you will choose a percentage that you wish to make. In our example, let's say you want to make a 50-percent gross margin. In our example, in 2008, it has been costing you $800. You will use the following formula to calculate your price.

Your price= Cost/(1-GM%)

Your Price=800/(1-.5)=800/.5=$1600

Now in 2009, it costs $900. What does your price need to be with this new increase?

Your Price=900/(1-.5)=900/.5= $1800

That is a $200 increase in what you need to be selling. This is a good way to calculate price. You can do this with any new product line you offer. Keep track of these numbers when you are reviewing your business at the one-, three-, and five-year mark. As you gain a reputation and experience, you can raise your margin incrementally.

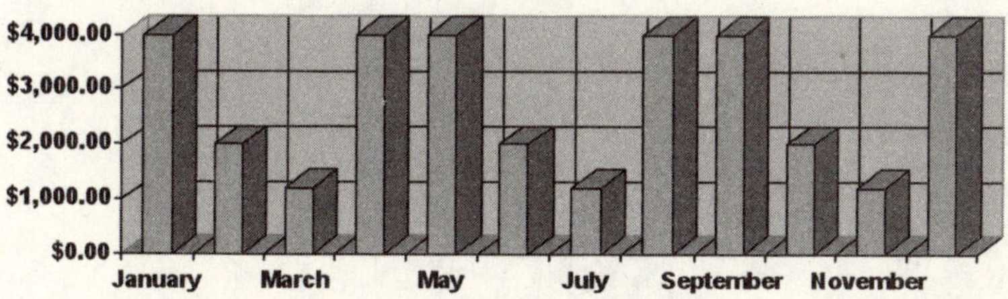

Gross Margin Yearly

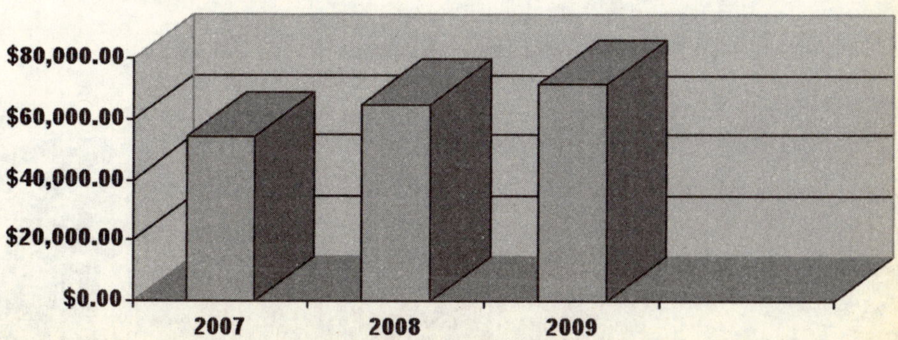

APPENDIX A

Case Studies

CASE STUDY: MICHAEL JORDAN

eBay ID: BullyStickGuy
www.BullyStickDrect.com
www.DogJerkyDirect.com
603-781-1674

Earning More Money with a Graduate Degree

I sell All Natural Dog Treats. My number-one seller is called a Bully Stick. I started selling items when I opened a Web site selling wholesale dog treats. I used eBay for the exposure. I thought I would just give it a try and see how it worked out.

eBay is where you go to get the best price on a product. Make sure you know your pricing and competition before you sell. Regular sellers are just using eBay instead of having a yard sale. PowerSellers are in it to make money and are running a business, either on eBay alone or in conjunction with another business.

You need to learn a lot of the shortcuts and ins and outs of eBay. It is a Web site with lots of content for the buyer and the seller. There are many tools that make your life easier if you know how to use them.

The most important aspect of my business is customer service, quality of product, and a 100 percent guarantee on returned product, which is of huge importance to any buyer. Running a business on an eBay site is quite easy.

CASE STUDY: MICHAEL JORDAN

As you build your business and you are selling more on eBay, the tools that are in place on eBay, as well as PayPal, provide all the information that can be exported to other sources. I take the financial data on a monthly basis to figure out fees, sales, and shipping. It is all broken down for you. The auto listing enables you to just monitor the listings and answer buyer questions.

I have two family members working for me, and sometimes I have friends' kids pack boxes and sort for me. Although I could use more help.

Even if you have a difficult time succeeding on eBay, make sure you have tried all aspects of the selling experience. eBay can be a finicky place. People like to have control. There are various styles of buyers. Some just want the product, some like beating someone else out. You need to have "Buy it Now" listings, as well as "auction" format.

I have people out bid an item in an auction format that they could get cheaper from me in a "Buy it Now" format. It happens all the time. Some people just like the satisfaction of "winning" the bid. I would encourage new sellers to read books on eBay PowerSellers. There are many aspects. eBay also offers classes.

CASE STUDY: CHARLENE ANDERSON

www.andersonshea.com

CLASSIFIED CASE STUDIES

directly from the experts

CASE STUDY: CHARLENE ANDERSON

I started with eBay in August of 1999. I began by selling things I no longer needed around the house... computer parts, sewing and knitting supplies, books; all sorts of odds and ends. That continued on for a few years, keeping the clutter down and a little cash coming in.

In 2002, I began selling as a salaried employee for a local video rental store. They had thousands of videos and DVDs that could no longer be rented. I sold all these unwanted videos and DVDs (over 10,000 of them). I was a PowerSeller after three months, and maintained it and 99.9 percent feedback in a very difficult category. I sold myself out of a job, and there were no more videos and DVDs to sell, so I was on my own.

It was at this time, 2005 or so, that I decided to get serious about opening a real eBay business; not just selling odds and ends, but selling a true niche of products. I chose a field I knew well (arts and crafts, as I also design professionally for art and craft magazines and books) and began sourcing, doing market research and the like. Three months after opening my business, I became a PowerSeller and have been one ever since. I'm proud of my 100 percent positive feedback as well. I treat customers like I want to be treated.

I run a strictly eBay business. I have tried my own Web store and a Vendio Web store and found that eBay works best for me. I sell tools and supplies for jewelry makers, beaders, knitters, and other artists and craftspeople. I sell everything from yarn and specialty pliers to torches for jewelry making.

I know a lot about the products I sell. I use them, and there is a good markup. There are not a lot of other people selling the same thing with the level of customer service I offer. For the most part, they are also easy to pack and ship. I also wanted to keep all inventory at home, so I looked for items that were small and easy to store in inventory.

It is fantastic being my own boss. All the successes are mine and all the failures are mine. Fortunately, there are more of the former than the later. I don't know if I could go back to working for someone else in a "real" office. I have no employees, just me. I enjoy working alone. If I have to be out of town, my husband does shipping for me, but I manage e-mails and other details on a MacBook Pro I take with me when I travel.

CASE STUDY: DANNA CRAWFORD

CEO/Founder PowerSellingMom, Inc.
PowerSellingMom.com
JoinMyNewsletter.com

CLASSIFIED CASE STUDIES™ directly from the experts

PowerSellingMom.com
Trading Assistant - Power Seller - Education Specialist
There is plenty of ebay for us all to be blessed and prosper

PowerSelling Mom.com

I started during the beanie-baby craze. I had heard I could sell them for more money on this place called "eBay" than I could at the local flea market. I Joined in 1997, and have been PowerSelling ever since!

I've grown into running a few different types of businesses under the umbrella of my main business, called PowerSellingMom, Inc. I'm an Education Specialist trained by eBay, teaching worldwide. I'm a blogger, and I do a lot of social marketing.

I'm what I call a "Treasure Hunt Seller." I've gotten very good at hunting out items from local yard sales and thrift stores. I sell all sorts of items. I'm also a Trading Assistant, which means I sell items for others, in addition to my own items.

CASE STUDY: DANNA CRAWFORD

The biggest obstacle I've had as an eBay seller is "Life." Meaning when life would throw me a curve ball I would have to adjust my eBay career around the event in my life. Such as when my father was diagnosed with cancer and only had nine months to live. I adjusted my eBay selling around a format so that I could make enough for the budget to get the bills paid. I lost my PowerSeller status and still managed to get by so that I could spend as much time as possible with my father and family. It was a challenge, but there is no other type of job I could have had that would have allowed me to drop everything and adjust so that I could continue to put my family first.

I have two employees, a virtual assistant, and a local assistant. I work out of my home office. I am my own boss, and I absolutely love it!

It sincerely breaks my heart when I hear from someone that wants to give up. First thing I explain: There is always a plan B. Sometimes you just have to take a step back and take a new look at what you are doing and how can you improve your style. Learn from mistakes and accept the challenge to succeed. Simplifying, organizing, and goal-setting have been the most important issues to my success.

Keep learning and looking for ways to improve. Carry on with each day as a continuing education. Look forward to each new lesson and thrive for success! PowerSellers work a bit harder to maintain the PowerSeller status. I do feel we are all united as PowerSellers, no matter what level of PowerSelling each may be at. We all work hard, and every PowerSeller I know works even harder as they climb up the PowerSelling ladder of success with anticipation of reaching the next level!

I've had many interesting items for sale, but one that I had a blast with was called the traveling toilet paper roll. I purchased it from a seller that had the idea for $11, and I sold it for $128. I am very good at promoting items, and this one I had a blast with. It brought me a lot of attention to my eBay store, in addition to growing my network of subscribers, and best of all, more eBay sales. I love to get creative with my eBay listings! I was trying to get the attention of Jay Leno, but had no luck. It was sold in August of 2006. I have the original auction available for viewing: **http://powersellingmom.com/pages/danna.html**.

CASE STUDY: JIM COCKRUM

SilentJim.com
SilentSalesMachine.com
MySilentTeam.com

Jim Cockrum lives in central Indiana with his wife of 14 years, and 5 children, ages 2 to 12. He is a full-time author, coach, entrepreneur, and eBay enthusiast.

I never intentionally set out to have a six-figure income from eBay and the Internet. I started out making a little side income, and it quickly grew into something that made me realize I may never have to have a "real job" again. I'm going on six years now without a "job." I'm working fewer hours per week than I ever have, and making more money.

For me, it all started with a few simple eBay auctions. I was thankful for those that helped me get started, giving me advice and tips, so to this day, I do the same thing myself.

I had an old pair of used Nike basketball shoes. I sold them on eBay for about $700 to someone in Singapore. I couldn't believe it when they actually paid for them! I was hooked! There's been no looking back since then!

On eBay, I've sold everything from event tickets to houses, and a little of everything in between. Right now, I have two full-time employees running the business, and things are going very well. I've gotten pretty good at finding liquidation deals, unusual high-profit items, and I'm also flipping real estate on eBay in a creative way that few have ever seen.

The houses I've sold on eBay were not sold for a final bid price, but instead, I make the bidding for the down payment only. This is a great way to make a killing on ugly houses because I set the price and act as the bank for the winning bidder. One of the most creative things I also sell is information products that bring in a very nice profit margin and sell quite well.

I read a lot. I still do. I love hearing how others succeed and improve their businesses on eBay and on the Internet. I guess the thing I needed most was confidence in the fact that someone really could have this life style. My wife and I have five kids to take care of, and she stays home with them because we home school. We are committed to that.

CASE STUDY: JIM COCKRUM

I can't afford to be "risky" with my business dealings. It has to work. After studying other online entrepreneurs, I gained the confidence to know that I could do this too. I got so much from those that taught me about online success that I've now made teaching a major part of my online business. I have a free newsletter that goes out to online entrepreneurs of all levels of success, and I teach them what I've found that works.

When I listen to my customers and give them what they want, and do it with excellence and creativity, they reward me with loyalty.

Here's an example:

Early on in my eBay career, I was getting several questions from my customers and others that found me online about how I was running my eBay and online business. I tried to keep up with the e-mail and questions, but it was too much for me to handle.

I recognized the fact that there were very few trusted leaders in this arena that were truly *walking the walk* by teaching *and* doing the business. Most of the other "teachers" weren't making a dime on eBay or the Internet!

I decided to write a book about my approach to eBay and Internet success, and that's when things really took off. The book was a simple word processing file at the time. I e-mailed it to people that inquired about it one at a time.

I started out giving the book away, but eventually, I started charging for it. That book is now in its 5th release and has sold about 60,000 copies. It's never been in hard-copy format — it's still a downloadable PDF file — but now it's sold day and night and automatically delivered instantly to all purchasing customers. My readers have always responded to the creativity of my "e-book." If you want to check it out, you can get it at **SilentSalesMachine.com**.

I now have a mailing list of about 100,000 online entrepreneurs that have signed up for my free e-mail-based newsletter as a result. The goal of that book started from my desire to help answer the questions I was getting about my creative approach to eBay and Internet success. To this day, nearly seven years and five updates later, that's still what it's all about.

This success has only been possible because I intentionally set out to

CASE STUDY: JIM COCKRUM

lead others. Instead of hiding my success secrets in the hope of keeping my competition away, I openly shared my success story and turned all potential competitors into customers!

There's no description that can express what it feels like being your own boss until you are living it. I've been doing it for six months almost to the day, and I still wake up some days and can't believe I don't have to "go to work." It's beautiful. What's even better is the fact that I've taught so many others the same opportunity. It's very rewarding.

As entrepreneurs, we live in the greatest time in the history of the world. It's never been easier to establish a truly global business. In under an hour, you can set up your first eBay item and be selling it to someone on the other side of the globe later that day. It's an amazing opportunity, and an amazing time to be alive.

Don't let any excuse keep you from pursuing your dream. There are plenty of good ideas out there just waiting for someone to pick them up and go for it. Having a job is just plain lazy if you have an entrepreneur's heart. Don't settle for boredom and a fraction of the pay that you are worth — get out there and make something happen!

The secret that has served me best in the six years that I've been working for myself is to always give customers what they want. Don't worry about what you think they need. Give them what you know for sure they *want.*

A great way to find out what they want is to grow an e-mail mailing list and then *ask them* what they want! It's a simple model that really works.

A PowerSeller could be someone that goes out and buys $10,000 worth of inventory and sells it all on eBay for $5,000. The title of PowerSeller is awarded based on sales volume only — not profit. It's a useless term. I'd much rather pursue using eBay as one small segment of my overall Internet marketing strategy and not worry about the title of PowerSeller. I happen to be a PowerSeller myself, but it's not a title I find rewarding.

I sold a few hours of one-on-one coaching time with me on eBay for $9,100! I was expecting bidding to go for about $2,000 or so, but I was blown away by how well it did. It's just more evidence that once you start having a little success doing anything online, the world is dying to hear how you did it, and they are willing to pay very well to get that advice!

CASE STUDY: JIMMY STEWART

Radio Computer Supply
176 Highlands Dr.
Woodstock, GA 30188
Cell 770-605-8764
Fax 770-216-1620

jim@RadioComputerSupply.com
www.RadioComputerSupply.com

CLASSIFIED CASE STUDIES™ directly from the experts

Back in winter of 1999, I decided I needed to clean out my basement of my electronics hobby. I decided, rather than throw it away, that maybe the old saying "one man's junk is another man's treasure" was true, so I decided to try it out. Much to my amazement, stuff that I was going to trash sold, so it all started from there.

I sell electronics, computer and networking parts, and books and media (DVDs & CDs). Most of my items are new, which I have obtained from businesses going out of business and liquidation sales.

I also sell a lot of used books that I obtain from yard sales and flea markets. I use a portable scanner and database on a PDA to find books in demand, rather than risking paying too much for a book that will only sell for $1 on eBay or Amazon.

I sell the products that I know about and that are/were part of my hobby, but now I also sell fiction books that I know nothing about except that they indicate a good find in the used book database.

CASE STUDY: JIMMY STEWART

Our greatest asset is customer service. We strive for the 5 STAR by treating the customer like I want to be treated. It is interesting that when I am a buyer on eBay and I do not get the same customer service as I try to give as a seller, it makes me look more at what I can do to even be better.

I run my business out of home. I have an office, a shipping room, and three storage rooms. I don't mind being my own boss. When things are clicking along, it is great. But then there are times when you have the customer that you cannot please, even if you offer to refund all charges. It would be nice not to have to deal with that.

If a seller is struggling, I would recommend that they join a local user group or Internet group, like OSI Rockstars (**www.osirockstars.com**), for guidance and support. They should also listen in on the eBay Internet radio programs, such as Ask Griff on **www.wsradio.com**, where they will hear how other people get around the hurdles.

One of the secrets of my success is knowing when and where to find the deals and then using the best customer service to bring back the customer. With every book I ship out, I send a nice, laminated bookmark with my URL listed so when they are finished reading the book, they know where to come back. I have received nice feedback just from that little feature.

Learn to live with the ups and downs in the eBay changes. Even for me, it is hard at times, but I force myself to wait it out. Business always looks greener on the other side, but there are ups and downs in every opportunity.

I once had an item (part of a radio) that I actually threw in the dumpster when I was cleaning the basement. I woke up the next morning with the thought "what if someone could use it," back to thinking of the trash versus treasure saying. I went out, dug in the dumpster, found it, listed it on eBay, and low and behold it sold for over $100. The guy who purchased it said he had been looking for this item for over five years and said it was a godsend that I had it. I do not know the other person's reason for wanting it that bid the price up, but I am glad he did. From this point on, I'll try to sell it before I trash it.

CASE STUDY: TOM ORR

Flex Wholesale
1029 N Wichita Suite 1
Wichita, KS 67203
888-318-4760

www.flex-wholesale.com eBay
www.flexwholesale.com Internet

I joined eBay in 1997. I started "hobby" selling shortly thereafter. In 2000, I was Vice President for a local ISP (Internet Service Provider) and we started an online auction/live auction business that we hoped would work well with eBay. We took consignments from local people and businesses and gave them the option of selling their merchandise via live auction or online through eBay. I've always been entrepreneurial minded. As soon as I saw the possibilities with eBay, I was hooked. That venture ultimately closed due to high overhead and lack of steady inventory.

In 2007, I started actively selling again on eBay. I started buying bulk electronics and operated out of my home. That November, we sold a family business, and I made the decision to do eBay full-time. I rented a 1,500 square foot warehouse and bought a full truck-load of return merchandise.

When I started full-time, I was buying returns. My last truck-load was all brand new excess inventory. The bulk of my inventory is currently shoes and apparel.

I love the shoes/apparel business. From a practical standpoint, they are small and easy to store and ship. From a personal point of view, people love to buy shoes and clothes. It makes them feel good. I love getting e-mail from customers who just got their order and are thrilled with their purchase. On a more selfish note, ladies love a man that has thousands of shoes! My biggest obstacle was finding sources for products to sell.

I feel one of the things that can help sellers achieve PowerSeller status is having a plan. It's important to approach an eBay business just like any other business. You need to have an idea of what and how you are going to sell. The nice thing about eBay is there are very few barriers to entry. If you don't have the money to buy inventory, you can start out selling other people's items.

CASE STUDY: TOM ORR

The most important aspect of my business is customer service and focus on doing what is important. There are many poor to mediocre sellers out there. It's not that difficult to stand out, but a passion for customer service is critical.

After being my own boss, I can't imagine it any other way. I probably put in more hours than the average person, but I don't feel like I "work" at all.

I would say that if selling on eBay or the Internet is something you really enjoy, don't give up! Getting started is the hardest part, whether it's a new job or working for yourself. Keep digging for information. Get active in networking with other sellers. One of the best things I have done is to join a seller's trade organization. I joined PESA (Professional eBay Sellers Alliance) and have found it to be an invaluable resource for growing my business and overcoming obstacles.

Be positive and stay flexible. eBay changes things quite often. Fees change, rules change. The marketplace is very different from when I first started selling. Each time major changes roll out, a group of sellers will fall by the wayside because they could not adapt to the changes.

Here are my top five tips for sellers:

1. Ship fast (same day if possible).
2. Focus on customer service.
3. Buy right.
4. Ask for discounts.
5. Stay positive. Don't take problem customers personally.

eBay can be a very gratifying place to sell. A while back, I sold a pair of shoes to a customer in Brazil. About two weeks later, he e-mailed me saying that he had not received them. I apologized to him and issued a refund. Sometimes, international packages get lost. That's just a part of doing business. Nearly a month later, the guy sends me his payment again. The shoes had just arrived.

APPENDIX B

Where eBay Began

When the Internet was relatively new, small business owners were incredibly excited over the concept of the "virtual store." Here, they thought they would finally be able to compete with larger businesses without needing to have tons of money and capital. They eagerly handed over the small price for Web hosting services and prepared themselves for the big money to start rolling in. However, most of them failed.

There was a time, not too long ago, when venture capitalists were throwing money at what came to be called dot-com companies. These companies, often without doing any market research to see whether there was even a need for their product, thought they were going to get wealthy overnight with their wonderful Web sites. They just assumed that people would find their store online and want to buy all their products because often, they were able to offer their services at much lower prices than the major retailers were.

The madness that ensued resembled the California Gold Rush of the 1800s, where potential prospectors streamed "en masse" to the west coast, following the allure of easy riches obtained by mining the wealth of gold lying unclaimed in the Rocky Mountains. Not many of them made much money, and many died before even seeing a real gold nugget. The dot-com boom had about the same amount of success. Not many ever saw their online stores become online successes.

The dot-com boom came and went in what has been called the dot-com bust. Hundreds of people went in droves, and since there was money to be had by investors longing for the promised, untapped riches of the online marketplace, many went for it, and ended in horrible failures.

Wary of the failure of the dot-com bust, many investors have become hesitant to put any amount of money into any kind of Internet business venture. Many still think that the lesson to be learned from the dot-com bust is to stay away from the online marketplace entirely.

Yet, in many ways, it is more feasible to make money online today then it has ever been. Much was learned from the mistakes of the dot-com era, and there are many more opportunities to be had today — real opportunities that are just waiting to be taken by determined, business-minded people.

Many people have heard the simplistic, not all-encompassing story that eBay started as a way for the founder's wife to add to her collection of PEZ dispensers. While it does have some basis in truth — the founder's then-girlfriend (later wife) was one of his inspirations for an online auction and one of the first sellers — the entire story is far more interesting and inspiring.

Pierre Omidyar was born in France in 1967 and immigrated to the United States with his family when he was a young boy. He was in junior high school when the first personal computers from companies like Radio Shack came on the market. Immediately, Omidyar had found his life's passion and what would become his life's work: the world of computers. His fascination with computers was too strong to resist; he frequently skipped physical education classes to sneak off and use a teacher's computer during those early years. Even before finishing college in 1988, Omidyar began an early career in programming and was involved in various businesses that specialized in programming for Macintosh and Apple computers.

In the early 1990s, "the Internet" was a catch phrase that was spreading like wildfire on the lips of every computer geek in Silicon Valley. The epicenter of all things computer in those days, southern California swooned at the thought of how the Internet was going to change the world, and all the money there was to be made doing it. Omidyar, too, was caught up in the excitement and even had some early Web sites devoted to such varied subjects as the Ebola virus and a university alumni site. But when it came to making money via the Internet, his ideals about business and the free market inspired him to pursue equality for the common man in purchasing. For instance, he had become wealthy at a young age by buying stocks prior to an initial public offering (IPO) and then benefiting when the stock gained significantly, just before the public had a chance to purchase it. This led Omidyar to wish that everybody would have the opportunity to buy low or bid the price up if the demand was there. He had been lucky with his shortcut to financial success, but he wanted to even the odds for everyone else.

While Omidyar could not do much to change the way the stock markets operate, he was able to incorporate his ideals into his own hobby that turned into the world's largest business foray the Internet would know in its early days. eBay was born in a quiet home office with little fanfare. Over Labor Day weekend in 1995, Omidyar wrote the basic programming that would operate a simple auction site and named it AuctionWeb. The site was hosted on his Web site, **eBay.com**, and shared space with the aforementioned mentioned Ebola virus information, and also a couple of pages used by his fiancée and the alumni Web site.

The auction format was simplistic and far from the neat, slick eBay most people think of today. The block lettering and grey background was rather boring, and there were only a few options: list an item, bid on an item, and view an item. It was plain functionality at its best. Attractiveness aside, users immediately fancied the new way to buy and sell. The first months of AuctionWeb were not blockbusters by today's standards, but by posting information about his new site on other Web sites and Usenet newsgroups (some of the earliest sites on the Internet), he was able to slowly build business. Within four months, thousands of auctions had been set up on

AuctionWeb, and the buzz about this new marketplace was spreading as quickly as the Internet itself.

Not content to merely provide a forum for buyers and sellers to do business, Omidyar made sure all users were aware of the ethical way he wished the site's users to treat each other. He posted a list of desired behaviors, such as being courteous and settling disputes politely. Thus were born the Community Values that today are still prominently featured in eBay's pages and discussion boards.

Initially, AuctionWeb charged no fees to the users, but when Omidyar's Internet service provider started complaining about his site's traffic, they forced him to bump up to a business account costing $250 per month. Hobby or not, that was a far cry from the $30 he had been spending, so the idea was born to charge just the sellers, not the buyers, starting in February of 1996. Users paid final-value fees through mail, sending checks, paper bills, or even coins taped together. Right from the start, the collected fees covered the new expenses, and even turned a small profit.

Omidyar knew he was on to something, and by the end of the summer of 1996, he quit his full-time job and devoted himself entirely to turning his once-hobby into a thriving business. Others who came on board, including Jeff Skoll, helped shape the site in its early years. One of Skoll's most notable contributions was convincing Omidyar to drop the other Web pages that were existent on **eBay.com** and stick solely to auctions. It was difficult, but Omidyar gave in and removed his prized Ebola virus page, along with the other non-auction pages from the site. From then on, AuctionWeb became known by the handle eBay.

The concept of eBay quickly caught on, and soon, many people thought of doing any type of commerce online as synonymous with eBay. Instead of hearing people say, "I bought this on the Internet," you were more likely to hear, "I bought it on eBay." It became the number one way of doing business on the Internet, and it still is.

By the end of 1996, eBay had almost 10,000 registrants and had sold over one million items. In 1998, eBay became a public company with its stock traded on the NASDAQ. Estimates in 2008 put the number of registered worldwide users at 222 million who were expected to buy and sell more than $40 billion worth of merchandise through eBay in 2009.

A recent study indicated that nearly 750,000 people in the United States rely on eBay for some or all of their income. While eBay has branched out to foreign countries, the United States is its most seasoned group of users and an important piece of its selling "pie." The gamut of eBay sellers runs from stay-at-home parents wanting to pad the family's budget to retired folks who know a thing or two about antiques. College students unload their old textbooks and computer junkies hawk their outdated equipment. But the fastest-growing segment of eBay sellers seems to be those who are making it into a real business, steadily earning at least a portion of their necessary income without ever leaving the comfort of their homes.

BIBLIOGRAPHY

Blacharski, D. & Lujanac, M. How and Where to Locate the Merchandise to Sell on eBay: Insider Information You Need to Know from the Experts Who Do It Every Day. Florida: Atlantic, 2007.

Blacharski, D. eBay's Secrets Revealed: The Insider's Guide to Advertising, Marketing, and Promoting Your eBay Store With Little or No Money. Florida: Atlantic, 2007.

Editors of Socrates, Business Plan Book, Advice From the Experts. Chicago: Socrates, 2006.

Peragine, J. How to Open & Operate a Financially Successful Wedding Consultant & Planning Business: With Companion CD-ROM. Florida: Atlantic, 2008.

Peragine, J. How to Open & Operate a Financially Successful Personal Training Business: With Companion CD-ROM. Florida: Atlantic, 2008.

Pinson, L. & Jinnett, J. Steps to Small Business Start Up, Everything You Need to Know to Turn Your Idea into a Successful Business. Chicago: Kaplan, 2006.

Russell, C. eBay Income: How Anyone of Any Age, Location, and/or Background Can Build a Highly Profitable Online Business with eBay. Florida: Atlantic, 2006.

Sitarz, D. Sole Proprietorship, Small Business Start Up Kit. 2nd Ed. Carbondale: Nova, 2007.

http://pages.ebay.com/help/basics/faq.html

http://pages.ebay.com/community/people/values.html

http://pages.ebay.com/services/buyandsell/powerseller/criteria.html

http://pages.ebay.com/help/policies/listing-links.html

http://www.uspto.gov/

http://pages.ebay.com/buyandsell/skype-viewitem/index.html?ssPageName=CMDV:AB

http://www.developer.ebay.com/programs/certifiedprovider/overview

http://codebase.ebay.com/programs/certifiedprovider/benefits/

http://www.irs.gov

AUTHOR BIOGRAPHY

John N. Peragine, Ph.D. is a writer and classical musician. John holds a B.S. in psychology from Appalachian State University. He loves to hike and spend time with his children. When John is not writing, he plays the piccolo with the Western Piedmont Symphony. His previous books, *The Complete Guide to Organizing Your Records for Estate Planning, How to Open & Operate a Financially Successful Wedding Consultant Business*, and *How to Open & Operate a Financially Successful Personal Training Business*, were also published by Atlantic Publishing Company.

INDEX

A

B

C

D

E

F

G

H

I

K

L

M

N

O

P

Q

R

S

T

U

V

W

Z